BESIDE THE SEA

Designed and Pieced by

LESLEY BRANKIN

Quilted by

Jan Chandler
(Quilting Solutions)

Happy Quilting!
Lesley Brankin

An intermediate/advanced level project using
Foundation Piecing techniques

V1

CONTENTS

Choosing Fabrics	3
Quilt Requirements	3
Using this Book	4
Making the Quilt	4
Basic Blocks	4
Section 1 - The Beach	5
Section 2 - Beach Huts & Shallow Waters	5
Section 3 - Rocky Coastline	6
Section 4 - Deep Sea & Seal Island	7
Section 5 - Above the Waves	8
Section 6 - On the Horizon	9
Section 7 - Up in the Sky	9
Section 8 - Lighthouse & Completing Top Section	10
Inner Sashing	10
Flag Borders	11
Outer Sashing	12
Quilting	12
Binding	13
Finishing Touches	13
Foundation Piecing - a Brief Guide	14

	Guidance Notes	Colour Plate	Templates
Basic Block	4		28
Basic Blocks Reversed & Half Diagonal	4		29
Beach Hut	16	32	30
Clam Shell	16	32	35
Crab	16	32	35
Cruise Liner	17	33	36-38
Dolphin	17	33	39-40
Fish - Large	18	32	41
Fish - Small	18	33	42
Lighthouse	19	34	43-47
Puffins	19	34	48
Seagull	20	34	49
Seahorses	20	32	50
Seal - Baby	20	34	51
Seal - Mother	21	34	52
Starfish	21	32	53
Sun	22	34	54
Trawler	22	33	55
Turtle	22	32	56
Whale	23	33	57-58
Yacht	23	33	59
Flag Blocks	24-27	31	60-64

Disclaimer

Every care has been taken to ensure the accuracy of these instructions, but no guarantee can be given with regard to the finished quilt as materials and procedures used will necessarily vary.

CHOOSING FABRICS

I had great fun in choosing appropriate fabrics for use in my version of 'Beside the Sea' and hope that you will too. It is not practical for me to specify all of the fabrics that I have used however, I have provided a list of suggested background fabrics (see Quilt Requirements) which you might find helpful.

For background fabrics I would recommend that you use non-patterned fabrics that will not compete with the block subjects themselves; plains or marbles are ideal. By contrast the feature blocks provide the opportunity to utilise specific fabric designs; tone on tones, marbles, batiks and small prints are all worth auditioning.

QUILT REQUIREMENTS

Quilt Dimensions: 63" x 81" approx.

Fabrics:

I have specified quite generous quantities of fabrics because foundation piecing techniques are used in this project. It is assumed that all fabrics are standard width (112 cm, 42"/44")

- ¾ m (30") sky blue, e.g. Misty (F1200-17) or Perfect Palette (Sky - 52)
- 1¼ m (50") turquoise, e.g. Fire & Ice (Fire Turquoise - F211-28)
- ¾ m (30") mid blue, e.g. Perfect Palette (Sea - 28)
- ½ m (20") jade green, e.g. Fire & Ice (Sea Green - F211-27)
- 1½ m (60") sea green, e.g. Reflections (Sea Green - F1222-14)
- 30 cm (12") pale grey, e.g. Fire & Ice (Ice Grey - F210-6)
- ¼ m (10") dark grey, e.g. Reflections (Black - F1222-21)
- 30 cm (12") purple, e.g. Perfect Palette (Hyacinth - 30)
- 60 cm (24") sand, e.g. Perfect Palette (Sand - 40)
- Small pieces of tone on tone and small pattern prints for feature blocks
- Fat quarter each of red, royal blue, yellow, black and white for flag blocks
- 60 cm (24") binding fabric, e.g. mid blue as above

The fabrics cited above are by Fabric Freedom.

Additional Needs:

- 70" x 90" backing fabric (allows for Long Arm quilting)
- 70" x 90" sized piece of wadding
- Stitch 'n' Tear or thin paper for paper piecing (e.g. cheap computer paper)
- Neutral sewing thread, e.g. grey YLI Soft Touch
- Decorative quilting threads
- Perlé embroidery threads
- A variety of buttons (¼" and ⅜" are ideal) and/or beads

USING THIS BOOK

Although my book provides instructions for the making of this endearing single bed sized quilt, the blocks can, of course, be made individually and used to create your own quilt and project layouts.

Apart from some of the flags, all of my blocks are designed to be foundation pieced. I have provided a brief overview of this technique (see page 14), however should you require more assistance many excellent books are widely available.

MAKING THE QUILT

A few hints before you start:
- A full colour block diagram is shown on page 31; this should be used as a General Layout Diagram for block placement and counts.
- Remember to press seam allowances as you proceed.

The Blocks
- Full instructions for each block can be found starting on page 16.
- When foundation piecing work with generous sized pieces of fabric - if you are too miserly you will find that frustration may rule the day!
- Allow a generous amount of fabric at the edges of the block - this provides plenty of scope when trimming blocks to their final sizes.

Sashings and Strips
- When cutting background strips you may need to join several smaller lengths of fabric together - the instructions given refer to the total joined length required.
- For ease of working, you may find it easier to cut sashing and strip lengths just slightly longer than needed - these can then be trimmed as you sew.

BASIC BLOCKS

Much of the central part of this quilt is constructed from a series of simple foundation pieced blocks interspersed with feature blocks. Four different variations of these 'Basic Blocks' are used.

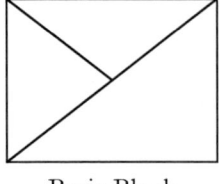   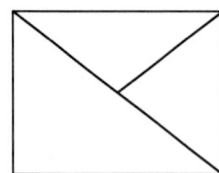   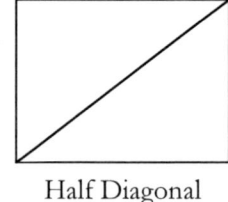   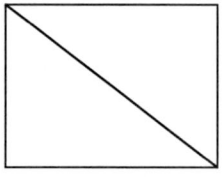

Basic Block | Basic Block Reversed | Half Diagonal Block | Half Diagonal Block Reversed

Each is constructed in the same way:
1. Copy the Foundation Block (page 28 or 29 as appropriate).
2. Foundation piece using appropriate fabrics (see following sections). If using a directional print, ensure that you align any linearity with the arrows shown on the foundations.
3. Trim finished block to 4½" x 3½".
4. Remove papers (can be done before or after trimming).

Section 1 - The Beach

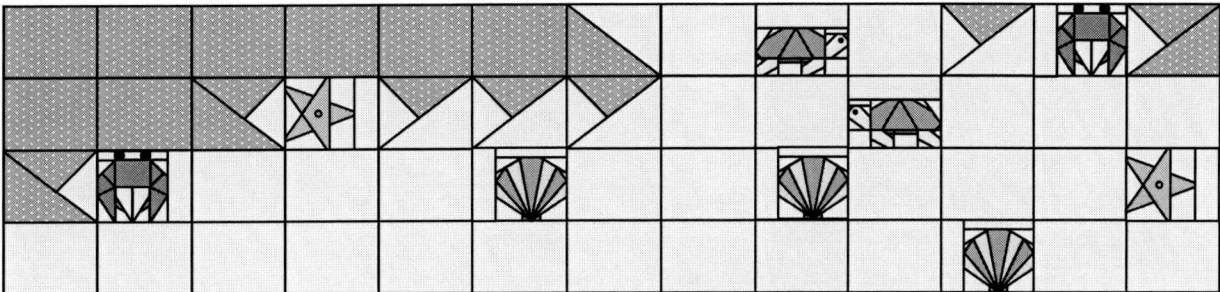

Figure 1 - Section 1 Construction

1. Using sand for the background, foundation piece the following feature blocks:
   - 2 Crabs
   - 2 Turtles (1 reversed)
   - 2 Starfish
   - 3 Clam Shells
2. Foundation piece the following Basic Blocks:

Block Type	make	fabric to use for piece 1	2	3
Half Diagonal Reversed*	1	sand	purple	n/a
Basic	1	purple	sand	purple
Basic	4	purple	sand	sand
Basic Reversed	2	purple	sand	purple

*use the alternate diagonal line as shown on template

3. In addition cut 8, 4½" x 3½" rectangles of purple fabric and 27 from sand.
4. Using Figure 1 for guidance, arrange the blocks to create a pleasing layout.
5. Join blocks together to make 4 long strips.
6. Join the 4 strips together.

Section 2 - Beach Huts & Shallow Waters

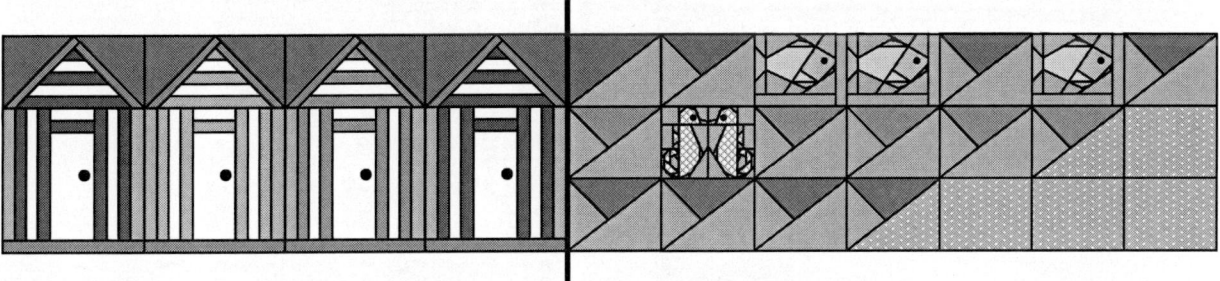

Figure 2 - Section 2 Construction

1. Using turquoise for the background, foundation piece the following feature blocks:
   - 3 Small Fish
   - 1 Seahorses

2. Foundation piece the following Basic Blocks:

Block Type	make	fabric to use for piece 1	2	3
Half Diagonal	1	mid blue	turquoise	n/a
Basic	6	mid blue	turquoise	turquoise
Basic	4	jade green	turquoise	turquoise
Basic	1	mid blue	turquoise	purple
Basic	1	jade green	turquoise	purple

3. In addition cut 4, 4½" x 3½" rectangles of purple fabric.
4. Using Figure 2 for guidance, arrange small blocks to create a pleasing layout consisting of 3 strips each of 7 blocks. Join blocks together.
5. Using turquoise and mid blue for the background, foundation piece 4 Beach Hut blocks.
6. Join the 4 Beach Hut blocks together.
7. Join the 2 subsections together.
8. Attach to top of Beach Section.

Section 3 - Rocky Coastline

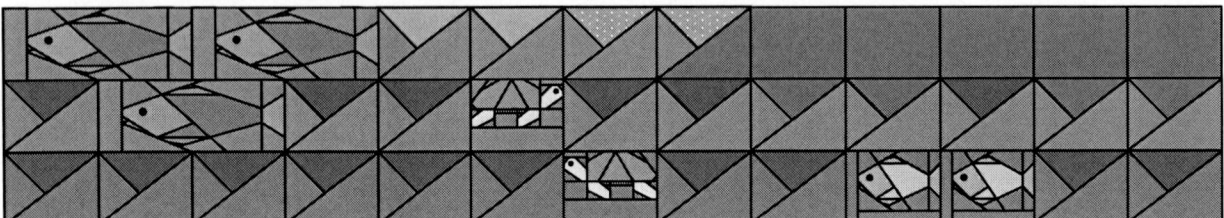

Figure 3 - Section 3 Construction

1. Foundation piece the following feature blocks:
   - 2 Small Fish (reversed) using jade green fabric for background
   - 2 Turtles, 1 using sea green and 1 using jade green (reverse turtle) for background
   - 3 Large Fish using sea green for background
2. Foundation piece the following Basic Blocks:

Block Type	make	fabric to use for piece 1	2	3
Basic	2	light grey	sea green	sea green
Basic	1	purple	sea green	sea green
Basic	1	purple	dark grey	sea green
Basic	6	mid blue	sea green	sea green
Basic	4	dark grey	sea green	sea green
Basic	10	mid blue	jade green	jade green

3. In addition cut 5, 4½" x 3½" rectangles of dark grey fabric.
4. Using Figure 3 for guidance, arrange blocks to create a pleasing layout.
5. Join blocks together to make 3 long strips.
6. Join the 3 strips together.
7. Attach to top of Beach Huts & Shallow Waters Section.

Section 4 - Deep Sea & Seal Island

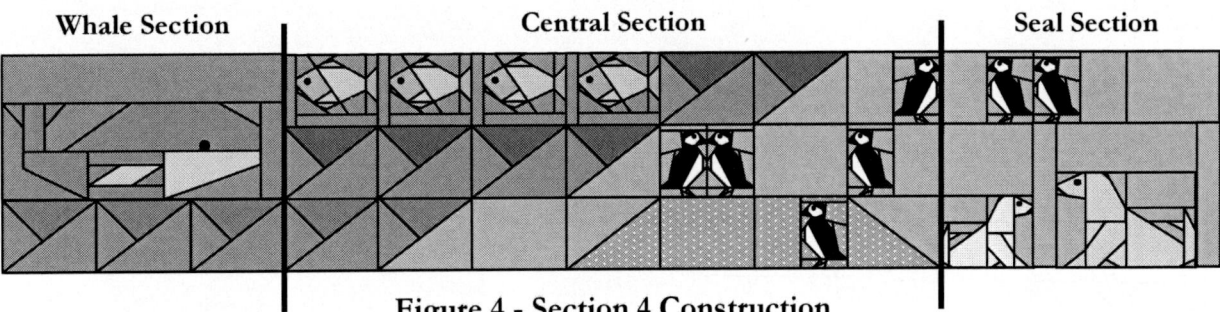

Figure 4 - Section 4 Construction

1. Using sea green for the background, foundation piece the following blocks:
   - 4 Small Fish (reversed)
   - 1 Whale
2. Using light grey for the background, foundation piece the following blocks:
   - 1 Baby Seal
   - 1 Mother Seal
   - 5 Puffin Blocks (for interest vary the number and orientation of puffins in each block)
3. Using purple for the background, foundation piece a further Puffin Block (with a single puffin).
4. Foundation piece the following Basic Blocks:

Block Type	make	fabric to use for piece 1	2	3
Half Diagonal	1	light grey	purple	n/a
Half Diagonal Reversed*	1	light grey	purple	n/a
Basic	4	mid blue	sea green	sea green
Basic	2	mid blue	sea green	light grey
Basic	4	jade green	sea green	sea green
Basic	1	jade green	sea green	light grey

*use the alternate diagonal line as shown on template

5. In addition cut 4, 4½" x 3½" rectangles of light grey fabric and 1 of purple.
8. Using Figure 4 for guidance, arrange blocks to create a pleasing layout.
9. Work as 3 subsections:
   - **Whale Section** - join 3 Basic Blocks to make a single strip. Attach to bottom of Whale block.
   - **Seal Section** - attach a light grey rectangle to top of Baby Seal. Join seal blocks together. Next, join 2 Puffin blocks and 1 light grey rectangle together to make a single strip. Attach to top of seals.
   - **Central Section** - join blocks to create 3 strips. Join the strips together.
10. Join the 3 subsections together.
11. Attach to top of Rocky Coastline Section.

Section 5 - Above the Waves

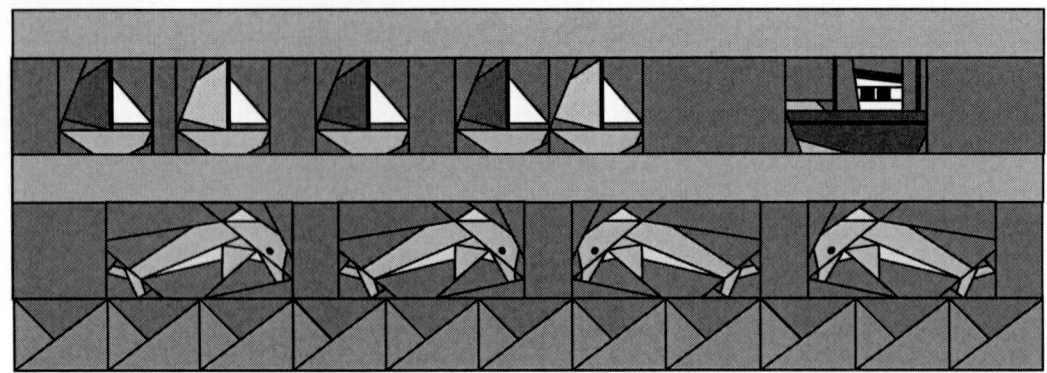

Figure 5 - Section 5 Construction

1. Using mid blue for the background, foundation piece the following feature blocks:
   - 4 Dolphins (2 reversed)
   - 1 Trawler
   - 5 Yachts
2. Foundation piece the following Basic Blocks:

Block Type	make	fabric to use for piece		
		1	2	3
Basic	11	mid blue	jade green	jade green

3. Join the Basic blocks to form a single long strip.
4. Cut the following rectangles from mid blue:
   - 1, 4½" x 4½"
   - 4, 2½" x 4½"

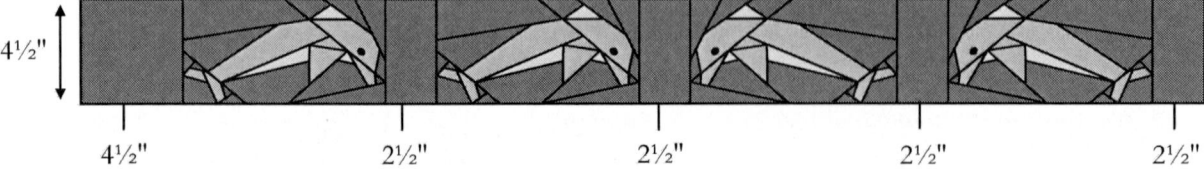

Figure 5a - Dolphin Subsection Cutting strips

5. Lay these out together with dolphin blocks as in Figure 5a. Join to make a single long strip.
6. Attach to top of Basic Block strip.
7. Cut the following rectangles from mid blue:
   - 3, 2½" x 4½"
   - 1, 1½" x 4½"
   - 1, 6½" x 4½"
   - 1, 5½" x 4½"

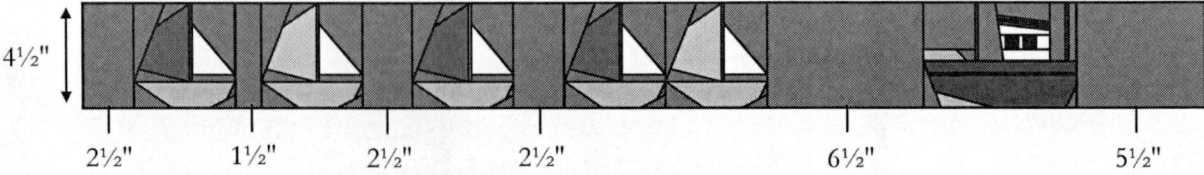

Figure 5b - Boat Subsection Cutting strips

8. Lay these out together with Yacht and Trawler blocks as in Figure 5b. Join to make a single long strip.
9. Cut 2, 44½" x 2½" strips of turquoise fabric.
10. Layer with Dolphin and Boat subsections as shown in Figure 5.
11. Join strips together.

Section 6 - On the Horizon

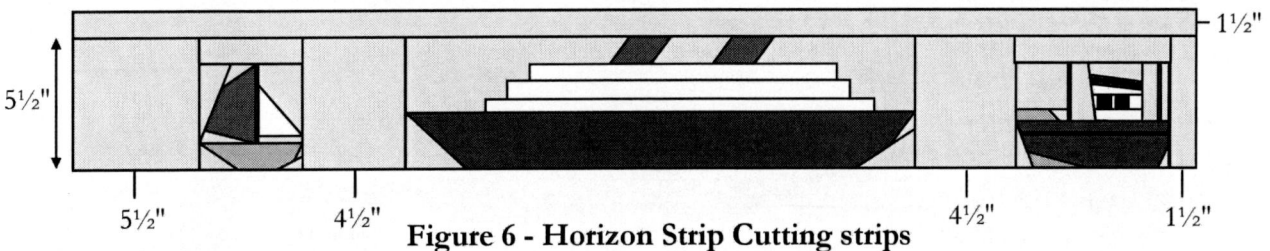

Figure 6 - Horizon Strip Cutting strips

1. Using sky blue for the background, foundation piece the following blocks:
   - 1 Yacht
   - 1 Trawler
   - 1 Cruise Liner
2. Cut a 4½" x 1½" rectangle of sky blue fabric and attach to top of Yacht block.
3. Cut a 6½" x 1½" rectangle of sky blue fabric and attach to top of Trawler block.
4. Cut the following rectangles from sky blue:
   - 1, 5½" x 5½"
   - 2, 4½" x 5½"
   - 1, 1½" x 5½"
5. Lay these out together with the boat blocks as shown. Join to make a single long strip.
6. Cut a 44½" x 1½" strip of sky blue and attach to top of boat strip.

Section 7 - Up in the Sky

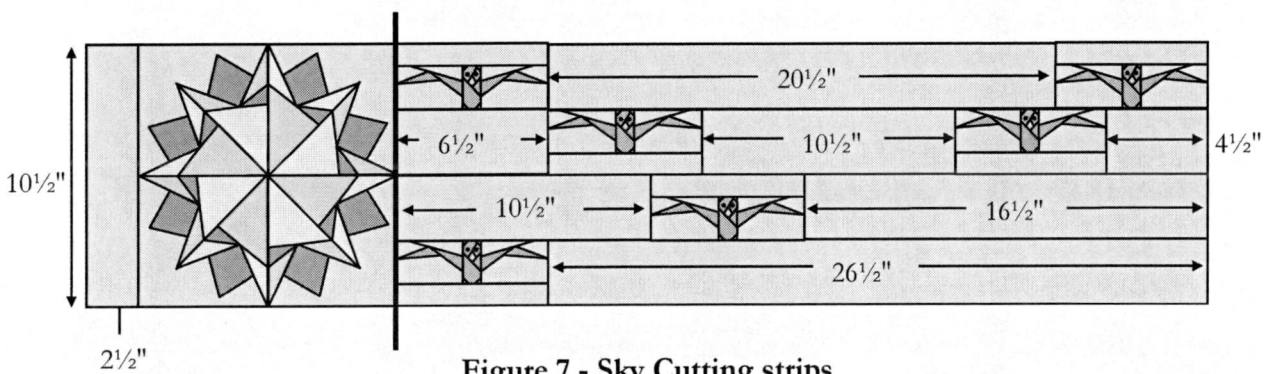

Figure 7 - Sky Cutting strips

1. Using sky blue for the background, foundation piece the following blocks:
   - 1 Sun
   - 6 Seagulls
2. Cut a 2½" x 10½" rectangle of sky blue fabric and attach to left side of Sun block.

3. Cut the following rectangular strips from sky blue:
   - 1, 4½" x 3"
   - 1, 6½" x 3"
   - 2, 10½" x 3"
   - 1, 16½" x 3"
   - 1, 20½" x 3"
   - 1, 26½" x 3"
4. Layout with Seagull blocks as shown. Join together to form 4 long strips.
5. Join 4 strips together.
6. Attach Seagull subsection to Sun subsection.

Section 8 - Lighthouse & Completing Top Section

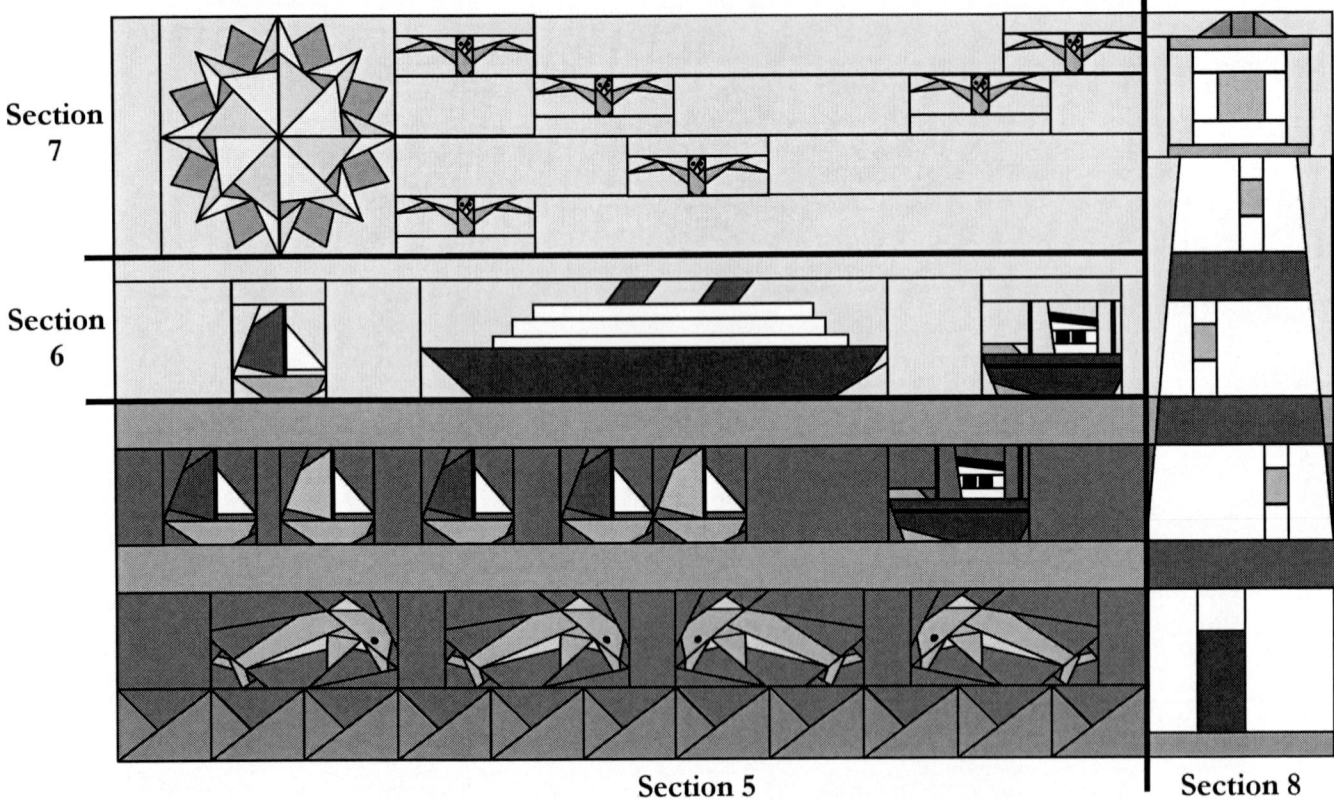

Figure 8 - Completing the Top Section of Quilt

1. Using sky blue, turquoise and mid blue for the background, foundation piece the Lighthouse block.
2. Join together Sections 5, 6 and 7.
3. Attach Lighthouse block (Section 8) to right of sub block.
4. Join to bottom section of quilt.

Measure your quilt top at this stage; it should be 52½" x 70½".

INNER SASHING

1. From sea green fabric cut two 1½" strips each totaling 54½" in length and two totaling 70½" (you will probably need to join smaller lengths).
2. Sew longer strips to either side of quilt.
3. Sew shorter strips to top and bottom of quilt.

FLAG BORDERS

There are four flag borders, each made up of nautical alphabet blocks, which are used to spell out a number of words. As instructions for all 26 letters of the alphabet, **Figure 9**, are provided you can tailor the lettering as you wish.

You will need blue, yellow, red, white and black fabrics for the flags themselves and turquoise for the background. If using a background fabric featuring a one-way design, e.g. waves, remember to consider the orientation of your fabric when cutting the dividing strips.

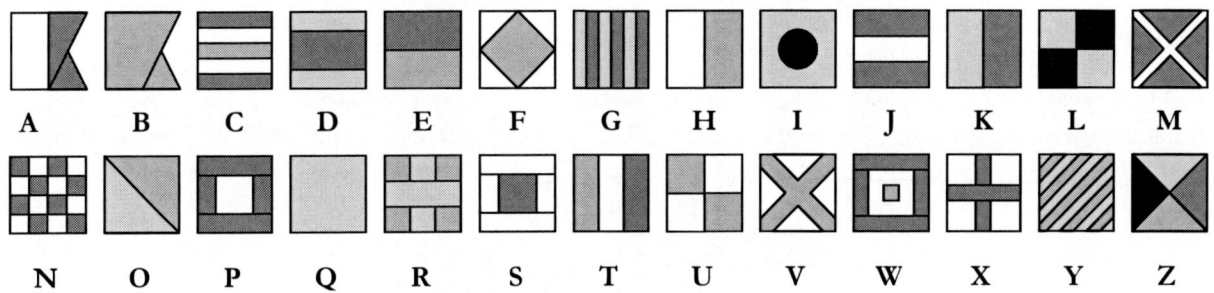

Figure 9 - Nautical Flag blocks
(See page 31 for a coloured version of this diagram).

1. **Left Hand Border** - Referring to the General Layout Diagram, page 31, make the following letter blocks (13 in total):

    OH I DO LIKE TO BE

    Cut the following strips from turquoise fabric:
    - 7, 3½" x 1½"
    - 5, 3½" x 5½"
    - 2, 3½" x 1"

    Lay out border strip as shown and join blocks together. The finished border strip should measure 72½" in length.

2. **Right Hand Border** - Referring to the General Layout Diagram, page 31, make the following letter blocks (16 in total):

    BESIDE THE SEASIDE

    Cut the following strips from turquoise fabric:
    - 13, 3½" x 1½"
    - 2, 3½" x 5½"
    - 2, 3½" x 1"

    Layout border strip as shown and join blocks together. The finished border strip should measure 72½" in length.

3. **Bottom Border** - Referring to the General Layout Diagram, page 31, make the following letter blocks (5 in total):

    QUILT

    Cut the following strips from turquoise fabric:
    - 4, 1½" x 3½"
    - 2, 21" x 3½"

Layout border strip as shown and join blocks together. The finished border strip should measure 60½" in length.

4. **Top Border** - Work out your own wording, it could be your name, the name of the recipient or whatever you wish. I used my name (LESLEY) and added an 'S'; 7 flag blocks in total.

Between each letter in a word insert a 1½" x 3½" (1" x 3" finished size) strip of turquoise fabric and a 5½" x 3½" (5" x 3" finished size) strip between any words. It is now necessary to calculate how much additional turquoise fabric is needed to make the total length of the top border up to 60½" (60" finished size) wide.

EXAMPLE
Note - the **finished** sizes of blocks and spacers should be used when calculating strip lengths

For my quilt I needed:

7, 3" x 3" flag blocks	21"
6, 1" x 3" letter spacers	+6"
0, 5" x 3" word spacers	+0"
Total	**27"**
Total width of strip required	60"
Less total from wording calculated above	-27"
Total length left to find	**33"**
Divide by 2 (creates 2 strips so wording will be centred)	16½"
Add ½" for seam allowances	+½"
Total length of 3½" high strips to be cut	**17"**

Therefore I needed to cut 2, 17" x 3½" strips of turquoise fabric to complete my border.

OUTER SASHING

From sea green fabric cut two 2½" strips each totaling 64½" in length and two totaling 78½" (you will probably need to join smaller lengths). You can use 2" wide strips if you wish but I prefer to use wider strips and allow myself plenty of leeway when later squaring up my quilt.

1. Sew longer strips to the sides of the quilt.
2. Sew shorter strips to top and bottom of the quilt.

QUILTING

1. Prepare the quilt sandwich. If you plan to have your quilting done on a Long Arm machine ensure that your backing is at least 3" larger all round than your quilt top (I suggest you use 70" x 90") or the size requested by your machinist.
2. Baste and quilt according to your personal preference.

'Beside the Sea' was custom long arm quilted. Although the outer edges of all feature blocks were 'stitched in the ditch' their centres were not quilted, thereby allowing them to 'stand forward' of the background. The background areas were quilted using a variety of appropriate quilting patterns.

In the borders each of the flag blocks was outline quilted and small nautical motifs included, where space permitted, in order to provide additional visual interest.

BINDING

1. Trim all sides of your quilt so that the layers are even, the corners are square and the outer border measures 1½" wide (gives a 1" wide sashing in the completed quilt). Your quilt will now measure approx. 63" x 81".
2. My quilt is edged with a ½" double binding. Cut sufficient 3" wide strips of mid blue fabric such that, when joined, they will go around the edge of the quilt, plus about 10" extra in length.
3. Join all strips together on the diagonal to make a single long strip.
4. Fold binding strip in half along the entire length, right sides outermost. Press.
5. Fold in ¼" along length of open long edge (both layers together). Press.

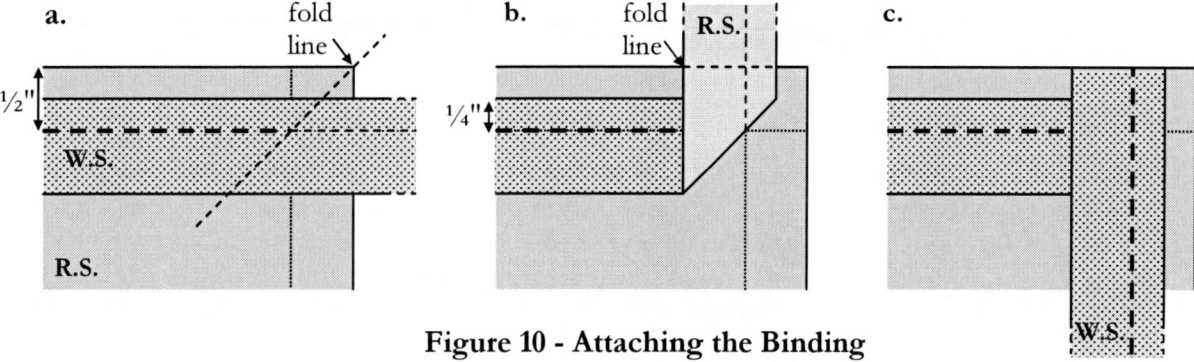

Figure 10 - Attaching the Binding

6. Referring to **Figure 10**, starting at centre of bottom edge and with right sides (r.s.) together, pin binding in place so that the ¼" fold line lies ½" in from the edge (you may find it useful to mark this line). Pin in place. Machine stitch along the fold line until approx. ½" from the corner (**10a**). Backstitch a little and remove quilt from the machine. Fold the binding strip up at 45° (**10b**) and then back down such that the fold aligns with the edge of the quilt and the ¼" fold line on the binding now lies ½" in from the next quilt edge. This gives spare fabric to fold over to the back of the quilt, ensuring neat corners.
7. Stitch along fold line, starting from top edge and thereby holding the mitre-fold in place as you sew (**10c**).
8. Continue sewing down the binding strip and forming corners until you return to the start. Fold in overlap edges to form a neat ending. Slip stitch down.
9. Fold the binding to the back of the quilt, carefully easing out any fullness at corners. Pin.
10. Hem along the seam line. Sew down mitred corners.

FINISHING TOUCHES

1. Add buttons and embroider any additional features as indicated in the relevant block instructions.
2. Don't forget to add that all-important label.

FOUNDATION PIECING - A BRIEF GUIDE

Foundation Piecing, also known variously as 'Paper Piecing' and the 'Stitch and Flip Technique', is a very accurate piecing technique where fabric patches are stitched to the reverse of a foundation block or unit (part of a block). Depending on the material used for the foundation, this can be either left permanently in place (e.g. lightweight cotton fabric or sew-in interfacing) or can be removed (e.g. paper or Stitch 'n' Tear).

The advantage of Foundation Piecing over the use of traditional piecing or template methods is that it allows you greater scope to piece more intricate designs. It can also be very quick to work once you become familiar with the technique.

Materials

You will need:
- Foundation paper, Stitch 'n' Tear or fine fabric e.g. calico or lawn
- Cottons or other fine fabrics e.g. silk
- Neutral coloured sewing thread

General Method

Patches are stitched to the blank side of the foundation. As such it is useful to have access to a light source (e.g. window or light box) to help position patches. Seam allowances are trimmed to size as the block is stitched so accurate cutting of the pieces is not necessary. When machine stitching, remember to use a slightly smaller stitch than usual especially if the foundation is to be removed.

First, the block or unit design must be traced or photocopied accurately on to the foundation and the order of stitching each patch noted. The design should appear in reverse to that of the finished block or unit.

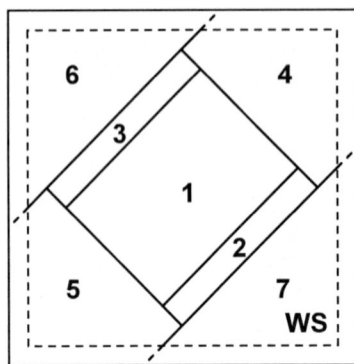

Foundation Template

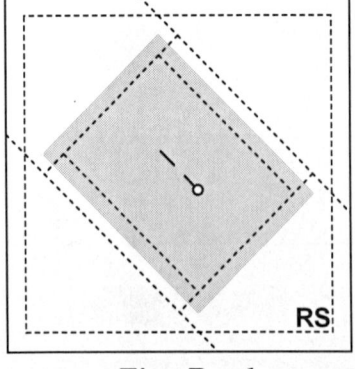

First Patch

Begin with the patch for area 1. Cut a piece of fabric slightly larger than the area to be covered and position this right side up, onto the blank side of the foundation covering area 1. Pin in place.

Next cut a piece of fabric that generously covers area 2. Place this right side down over patch 1, aligning the corresponding allowance edge. To help with placement of fabric, mark each end of the stitching line with a pin. Pin patch 2. Turn the foundation over and stitch along the line between patch 1 and 2 starting and finishing a few stitches beyond the marked line.

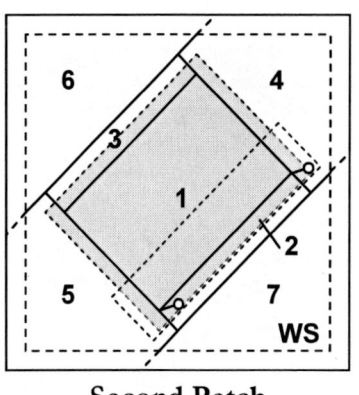
Second Patch

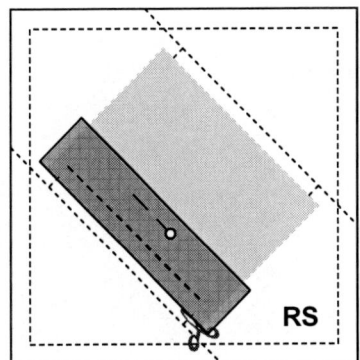
Trim Fabric Allowance

Turn unit over and trim seam allowances.

Flip patch 2 so that the right side of the fabric is now visible and press flat.

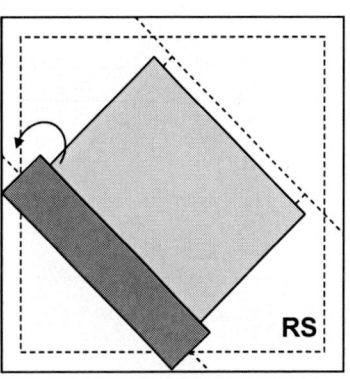
Flip and Press

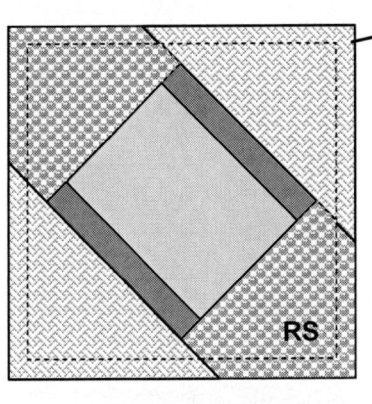
Finished Unit

Trim unit allowance to ¼"

Continue to stitch patches in numerical order, making sure that the fabric extends over the seam allowance around the outer edge of the unit. When the unit is complete, trim back seam allowances to a neat ¼".

Sewing Units Together

Units are sewn together with a ¼" seam allowance as they would be for any traditionally pieced patchwork technique. If units are different shapes then follow the construction order given in the instructions.

Papers need to be removed - this can be done once a unit has been trimmed to its accurate size or it can be done after units have been joined.

Fabric foundations can be left in if desired.

BEACH HUT

Block Size: 6" x 9" (make 4)

You will need:
- background - mid blue, turquoise
- hut - grey, white and choice of paint colour, e.g. red, jade green, pale blue
- button - 1 x ¼" for handle

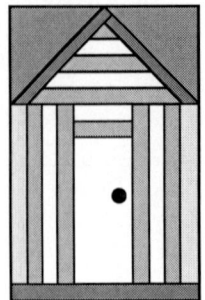

Making a Block
1. Copy Beach Hut Foundation block.
2. Foundation piece using appropriate colours.
3. Trim finished block to 6½" x 9½".
4. Remove papers (can be done before or after trimming).

Finishing (completed after quilting)
1. Sew on button for door handle.

CLAM SHELL

Block Size: 4" x 3" (make 3)

You will need:
- background - sand
- shell - 2 contrasting shades

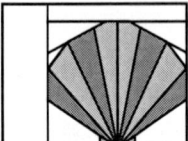

Making a Block
1. Copy Foundation Units A and B.
2. Foundation piece both Units using sand for background.
3. Join Unit A to B as shown.

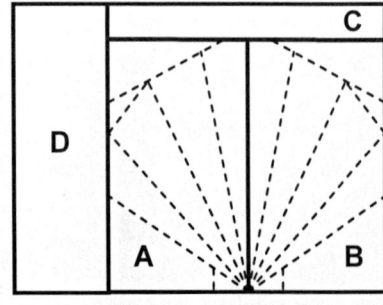

Unit Placement
(right sides facing)

4. Cut a 3½" x ⅞" strip of background fabric (Unit C) and referring to Unit Placement diagram sew to top of shell sub-block.
5. Cut a 1½" x 3½" strip of background fabric (Unit D) and sew to one side of shell sub-block (either side as preferred).
6. Trim finished block to 4½" x 3½".
7. Remove papers (can be done before or after trimming).

CRAB

Block Size: 4" x 3" (make 2)

You will need:
- background - sand
- crab - orange
- buttons - 2 x ⅜" black

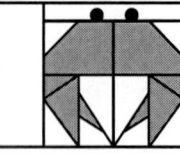

Making a Block
1. Copy Foundation Units A and B.
2. Foundation piece both Units using sand for background.
3. Referring to Unit Placement diagram, join Unit A to B.

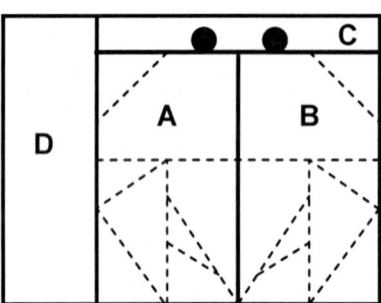

Unit Placement
(right sides facing)

4. Cut a 3½" x ⅞" strip of background fabric (Unit C) and sew to the top of crab sub-block.
5. Cut a 1½" x 3½" strip of background fabric (Unit D) and sew to one side of crab sub-block (either side as preferred).
6. Trim finished block to 4½" x 3½".
7. Remove papers (can be done before or after trimming).

Finishing (completed after quilting)
1. Sew on buttons for eyes.

CRUISE LINER

Block Size: 20" x 5" (make 1)

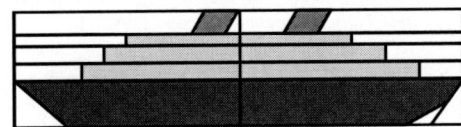

You will need:
- background - sky blue
- liner - white, red, grey
- small anchor (optional)

Making a Block

1. Copy Foundation Units A1 through D1 and A2 through D2.
2. Join Unit A1 to A2, B1 to B2, C1 to C2 and D1 to D2.
3. Foundation piece all 4 Units using sky blue for background.
4. Referring to Unit Placement diagram, join Units.

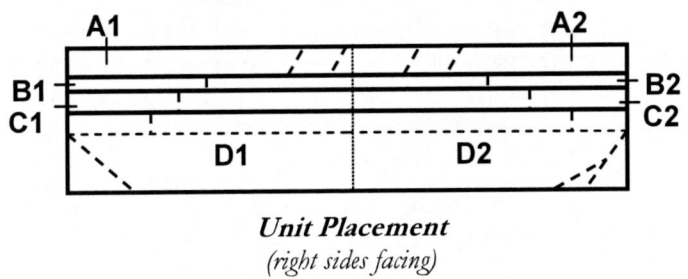

Unit Placement
(right sides facing)

5. Trim finished block to 20½" x 5½".
6. Remove papers (can be done before or after trimming).

Finishing (completed after quilting)

1. Sew on anchor button.

TIP
Before removing papers score along stitching lines with the back of a stitch ripper.

This makes it easier to remove the papers afterwards.

DOLPHIN

Block Size: 8" x 4" (make 4 - 2 reversed)

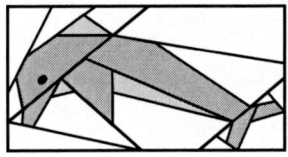

You will need:
- background - mid blue
- dolphin - 2 shades of grey
- button - 1 x ¼" black

Making a Block

1. Copy Foundation Units A through D.
2. Foundation piece all 4 Units using mid blue for background.
3. Referring to Unit Placement diagram, join Unit A to B and then attach Unit C. Finally, attach Unit D.

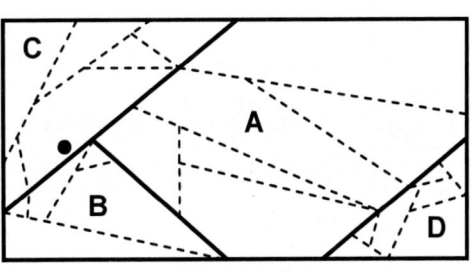

Unit Placement
(right sides facing)

4. Trim finished block to 8½" x 4½".
5. Remove papers (can be done before or after trimming).

Finishing (completed after quilting)

1. Sew on button for eye.

TIP
Press and trim seam allowances each time a new piece is added to a block.

This assists with ensuring accuracy and reduces bulk.

FISH - LARGE

Block Size: 8" x 3" (make 3)

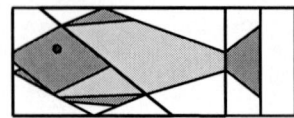

You will need:
- background - sea green
- fish - 2 shades
- button - 1 x ⅜" black

Making a Block

1. Copy Foundation Units A through C.
2. Foundation piece all 3 Units using sea green for background.
3. Referring to Unit Placement diagram, join Unit A to B and then attach Unit C.

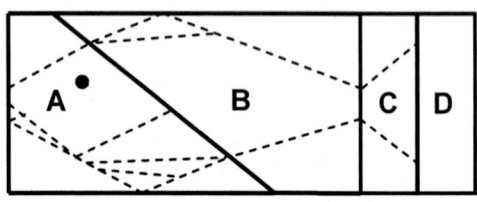

Unit Placement
(right sides facing)

4. Cut a 1½" x 3½" strip of background fabric (Unit D) and sew this to one side of the fish sub-block (either side as preferred).
5. Trim finished block to 8½" x 3½".
6. Remove papers (can be done before or after trimming).

Finishing (completed after quilting)

1. Sew on button for eye.

> ***TIP***
> *Remove papers in the opposite numerical order to that used when sewing i.e. remove the last piece first.*
>
> *This makes it much easier to remove papers fully.*

FISH - SMALL

Block Size: 4" x 3" (make 9 - 6 reversed)

You will need:
- background - sea green, turquoise or jade green
- fish - 2 shades
- button - 1 x ¼" white e.g. shirt button

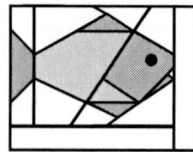

Making a Block

1. Copy Foundation Units A through C, using the normal or reversed template as relevant.
2. Foundation piece all 3 Units using appropriate colours for background.
3. Referring to Unit Placement diagram, join Unit A to B and then attach Unit C.

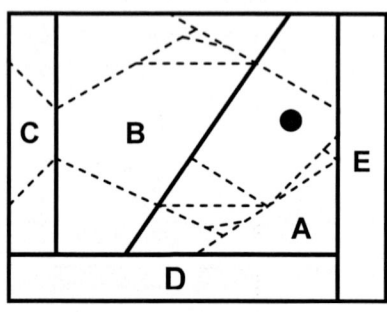

Unit Placement
(right sides facing)

4. Cut a 4" x 1" strip of background fabric (Unit D) and sew this to the top or bottom of the fish sub-block as preferred.
5. Cut a 1" x 3½" strip of background fabric (Unit E) and sew to one side of fish (either side as preferred).
6. Trim finished block to 4½" x 3½".
7. Remove papers (can be done before or after trimming).

Finishing (completed after quilting)

1. Sew on button for eye.

> ***TIP***
> *Use as fine a thread as possible for piecing.*
>
> *This helps reduce bulk.*

LIGHTHOUSE

Block Size: 8" x 31" (make 1)

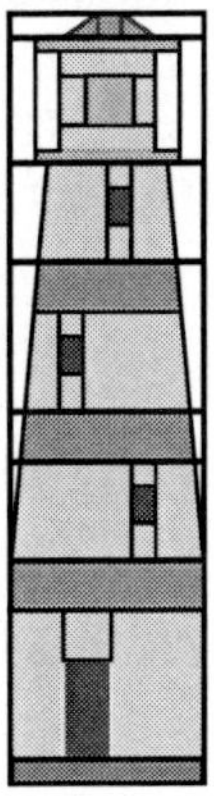

You will need:
- background - sky blue, mid blue and turquoise
- lighthouse - white, greys, red, black, brown, yellow
- button - 1 x ¼" brown for handle

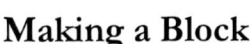

Making a Block

1. Copy Foundation Unit B and Units D through I.
2. Foundation piece Unit B.
3. Cut an 8½" x 1½" piece of grey fabric (Unit A) and attach to bottom of Unit B.
4. Cut an 8½" x 2½" piece of red fabric (Unit C) and attach to top of Unit B.
5. Foundation piece Units F through I using sky blue for background, Unit D using mid blue and E using turquoise.
6. Referring to Unit Placement diagram, join blocks in order shown.
7. Trim finished block to 8½" x 31½".
8. Remove papers (can be done before or after trimming).

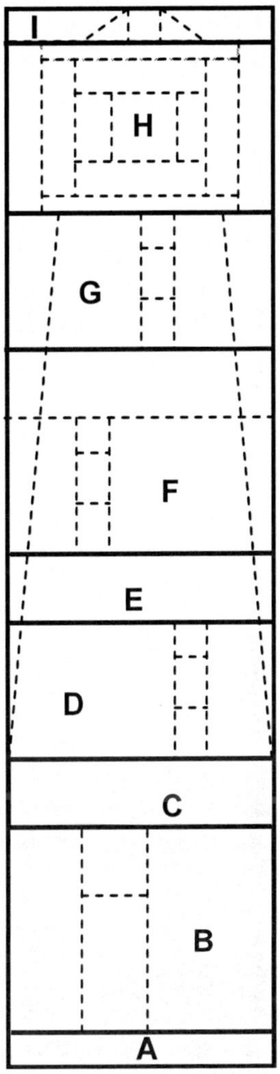

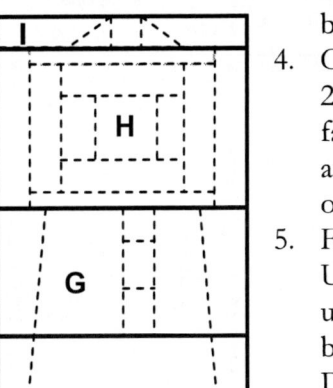

Unit Placement
(right sides facing)

Finishing (completed after quilting)

1. Sew on button for door handle.

PUFFINS or PUFFIN

Block Size: 4" x 3" (make 6)

You will need:
- background - pale grey or purple
- puffin - black, white, orange, red, blue
- bead - 1 black per puffin

Making a Block

1. Copy Foundation Units A through F or A through C if only making one puffin.
2. Using pale grey or purple for background foundation piece 3 or 6 Units as appropriate.
3. Referring to Unit Placement diagram, join Unit B to A, then add C (and similarly if appropriate Unit E to D and then add F).

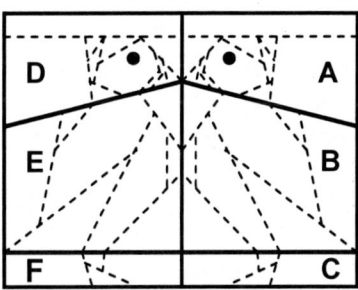

Unit Placement
(right sides facing)

4. If making a block with only 1 puffin then cut a 2½" x 3½" piece of grey or purple and attach to one side of puffin sub-block.
5. Trim finished block to 4½" x 3½".
6. Remove papers (can be done before or after trimming).

Finishing (completed after quilting)

1. Sew on bead(s) for eye(s).

> **TIP**
> *Reduce the machine stitch length when foundation piecing.*
>
> *This makes it easier to remove the papers afterwards.*

SEAGULL

Block Size: 6" x 2½" (make 6)

You will need:
- background - sky blue
- seagull - white, orange
- beads - 2 x black
- thread - orange perlé (optional)

Making a Block

1. Copy foundation Units A through C.
2. Foundation piece all 3 Units using sky blue for background.
3. Referring to Unit Placement diagram, join Units B and C to either side of Unit A.

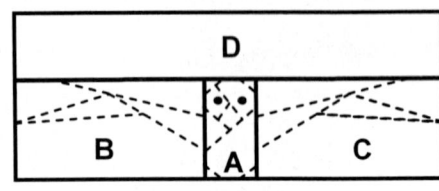

Unit Placement
(right sides facing)

8. Cut a 6½" x 1½" strip of sky blue fabric (Unit D) and sew this to the top or bottom of the seagull sub-block as preferred.
4. Trim finished block to 6½" x 3".
5. Remove papers (can be done before or after trimming).

Finishing (completed after quilting)

1. Sew on beads for eyes.
2. Optionally, using orange perlé thread, embroider feet on the seagulls.

SEAHORSES

Block Size: 4" x 3" (make 1)

You will need:
- background - turquoise
- seahorse - 2 colours
- beads - 2 x black

Making a Block

1. Copy Foundation Units A through H.
2. Foundation piece all 8 Units using turquoise for background.
3. Referring to Unit Placement diagram, join Unit C to D. Then attach Unit B. Now attach Unit A.
4. Referring to Unit Placement diagram, join Unit G to H. Then attach to Unit F. Now attach Unit E.

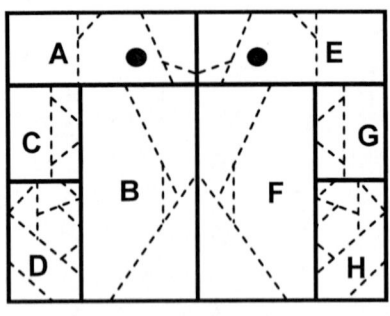

Unit Placement
(right sides facing)

5. Join seahorse sub-blocks together.
6. Trim finished block to 4½" x 3½".
7. Remove papers (can be done before or after trimming).

Finishing (completed after quilting)

1. Sew on beads for eyes.

SEAL - BABY

Block Size: 4" x 3" (make 1)

You will need:
- background - pale grey
- seal - cream
- button - 1 x ¼" black
- thread - cream perlé

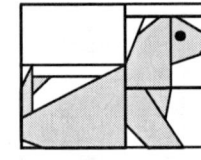

Making a Block

1. Copy Foundation Units A through C.
2. Foundation piece all 3 Units using pale grey for background.
3. Referring to Unit Placement diagram, join Unit A to B. Attach Unit C.

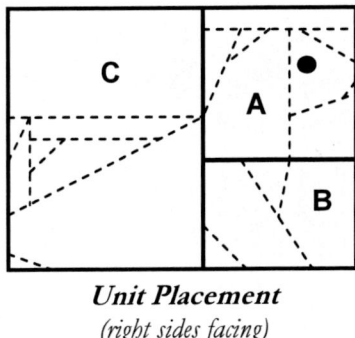

Unit Placement
(right sides facing)

4. Trim finished block to 4½" x 3½".
5. Remove papers (can be done before or after trimming).

Finishing (completed after quilting)

1. Sew on button for eye.
2. Optionally embroider some whiskers on the seal using a straight stitch.

SEAL - MOTHER

Block Size: 8" x 6" (make 1)

You will need:
- background - pale grey
- seal - grey
- button - 1 x ⅜" black
- thread - grey perlé

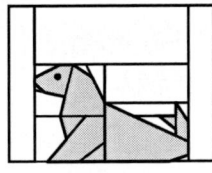

Making a Block

1. Copy Foundation Units A through C.
2. Foundation piece all 3 Units using pale grey for background.
3. Referring to Unit Placement diagram, join Unit A to B and then add Unit C.

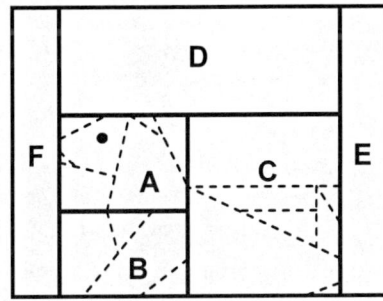

Unit Placement
(right sides facing)

4. Cut a 6½" x 2¾" strip of pale grey fabric (Unit D) and sew on top of seal sub-block.
5. Cut 2, 1½" x 6½" strips of pale grey fabric (Units E and F) and sew one to either side of seal sub-block.
6. Trim finished block to 8½" x 6½".
7. Remove papers (can be done before or after trimming).

Finishing (completed after quilting)

1. Sew on button for eye.
2. Optionally embroider some whiskers on the seal using a straight stitch.

STARFISH

Block Size: 4" x 3" (make 2)

You will need:
- background - sand
- starfish - rusty brown
- button - 1 x ⅜" brown

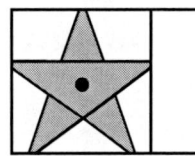

Making a Block

1. Copy Foundation Units A through C.
2. Foundation piece all 3 Units using sand for background.
3. Referring to Unit Placement diagram, join Unit A to B and then add Unit C.

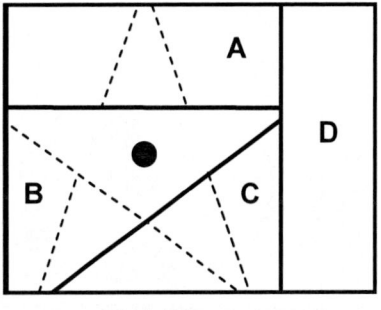

Unit Placement
(right sides facing)

4. Cut a 1½" x 3½" strip of sand fabric (Unit D) and sew to one side of starfish sub-block (either side as preferred).
5. Trim finished block to 4½" x 3½".
6. Remove papers (can be done before or after trimming).

Finishing (completed after quilting)

1. Sew on button for mouth.

SUN

Block Size: 10" x 10" (make 1)

You will need:
- background - sky blue
- sun - a variety of yellows and oranges

Making a Block
1. Make 4 copies each of Foundation Units A and B.
2. Foundation piece a Unit A and a Unit B using sky blue for backgrounds.
3. Referring to Unit Placement diagram, join a Unit A to a Unit B.

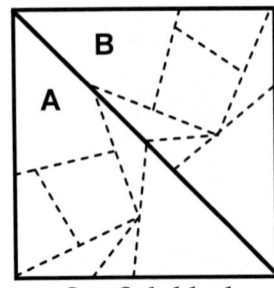 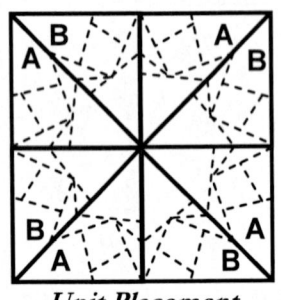

Sun Sub-block
(right sides facing)

Unit Placement
(right sides facing)

4. Repeat steps 2. and 3. a further 3 times and then join sub-blocks together as shown.
5. Trim finished block to 10½" x 10½".
6. Remove papers (can be done before or after trimming).

TRAWLER

Block Size: 6" x 4" (make 2)

You will need:
- background - sky blue or mid blue
- trawler - black, white, red, grey
- small anchor button (optional)
- thread - black perlé thread

Making a Block
1. Copy Foundation Units A through D.
2. Foundation piece all 4 Units using either sky blue or mid blue for background.
3. Referring to Unit Placement diagram, join Units A and C to B. Join this sub-block to Unit D.

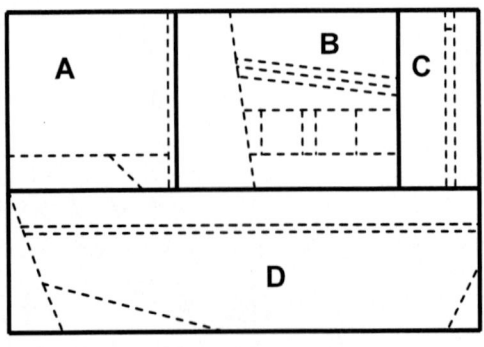

Unit Placement
(right sides facing)

4. Trim finished block to 6½" x 4½".
5. Remove papers (can be done before or after trimming).

Finishing (completed after quilting)
1. Sew on anchor.
2. Using black perlé thread embroider lines of rigging.

TURTLE

Block Size: 4" x 3" (make 4 - 2 reversed)

You will need:
- background - sand, jade green or sea green
- turtle - green, cream
- bead - 1 x ¼" black

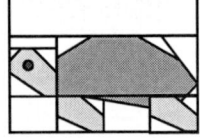

Making a Block
1. Copy Foundation Units A through D.
2. Foundation piece all 4 Units using sand, jade green or sea green for background.
3. Referring to Unit Placement diagram, join Unit A and B. Join to Unit C and then attach Unit D.

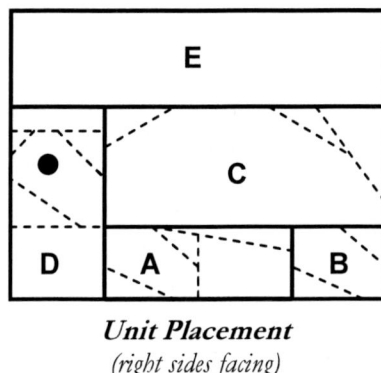

Unit Placement
(right sides facing)

4. Cut a 4½" x 1½" strip of background fabric (Unit E) and sew to top or bottom of turtle sub-block (either side as preferred).
5. Trim finished block to 4½" x 3½".
6. Remove papers (can be done before or after trimming).

Finishing (completed after quilting)

1. Sew on bead for eye.

WHALE

Block Size: 12" x 6" (make 1)

You will need:
- background - sea green
- whale - 2 shades of grey
- button - 1 x ⅜" black

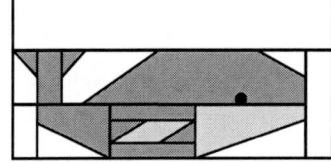

Making a Block

1. Copy Foundation Units A through D.
2. Foundation piece all 4 Units using sea green for background.
3. Referring to Unit Placement diagram, join Unit B to A and C to D. Join sub-blocks together as shown.

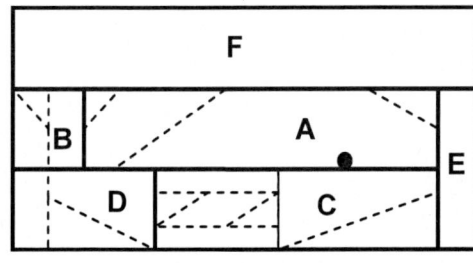

Unit Placement
(right sides facing)

4. Cut a 4½" x 1½" strip of background fabric (Unit E) and sew to right of whale sub-block.
5. Cut a 12½" x 2½" strip of background fabric (Unit F) and sew to top of whale sub-block.
6. Trim finished block to 12½" x 6½".
7. Remove papers (can be done before or after trimming).

Finishing (completed after quilting)

1. Sew on button for eye.

YACHT

Block Size: 4" x 4" (make 6)

You will need:
- background - sky blue or mid blue
- yacht - white, grey, brown, red or blue

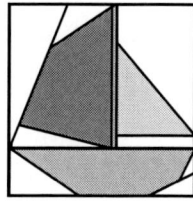

Making a Block

1. Copy Foundation Units A through C.
2. Foundation piece all 3 Units using sky blue or mid blue for background.
3. Referring to Unit Placement diagram, join Units A to Unit B. Attach to Unit C.

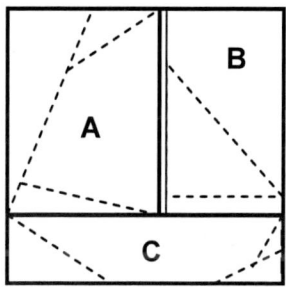

Unit Placement
(right sides facing)

4. Trim finished block to 4½" x 4½".
5. Remove papers (can be done before or after trimming).

FLAG BLOCKS

All blocks are 3" x 3" finished size.

Letter A - foundation pieced

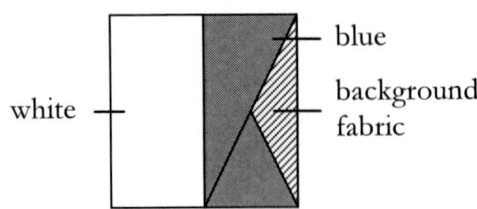

1. Using blue and white fabrics (and turquoise for background) piece block.
2. Trim to an accurate 3½" x 3½" square.
3. Remove papers.

Letter B - foundation pieced

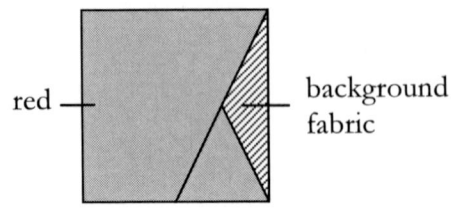

1. Using red fabric (and turquoise for background) piece block.
2. Trim to an accurate 3½" x 3½" square.
3. Remove papers.

Letter C - foundation pieced

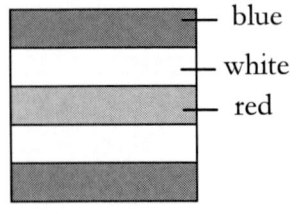

1. Using blue, white and red fabrics piece block.
2. Trim to an accurate 3½" x 3½" square.
3. Remove papers.

Letter D - traditionally pieced

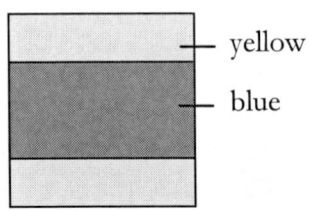

1. Cut 2, 3½" x 1¼" yellow rectangles.
2. Cut a 3½" x 2" blue rectangle.
3. Lay out pieces as shown.
4. Sew together. Press.

Letter E - traditionally pieced

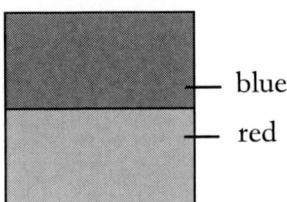

1. Cut a 3½" x 2" rectangle each of blue and red.
2. Lay out pieces as shown.
3. Sew together. Press.

Letter F - foundation pieced

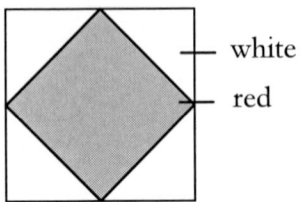

1. Using red and white fabrics piece block.
2. Trim to an accurate 3½" x 3½" square.
3. Remove papers.

Letter G - traditionally pieced

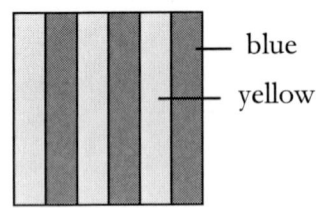

1. Cut 3, 1" x 3½" rectangles each of yellow and blue.
2. Lay out pieces as shown.
3. Sew together. Press.

Letter H - traditionally pieced

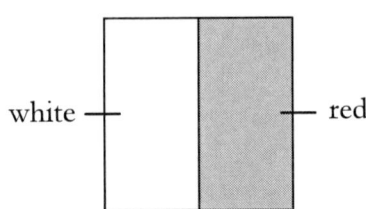

1. Cut a 2" x 3½" rectangle each of white and red.
2. Lay out pieces as shown.
3. Sew together. Press.

Letter I - appliquéd

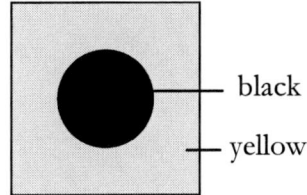

1. Cut a 4" x 4" yellow square.
2. Cut a 2½" diameter black circle.
3. Cut a 1¾" diameter circle from thin card.
4. Baste around edge of fabric circle. Place card template in centre. Pull up threads and securely tie off.
5. Centre circle on yellow fabric. Pin in place.
6. Stitch circle on (by hand or machine).
7. Neatly cut away excess yellow fabric from back of block.
8. Press.
9. Ensuring circle is centred, trim block to an accurate 3½" x 3½" square.

Letter J - traditionally pieced

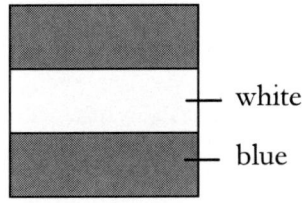

1. Cut 2, 3½" blue rectangles.
2. Cut a 3½" x 1½" white rectangle.
3. Lay out pieces as shown and sew together.
4. Press.

Letter K - traditionally pieced

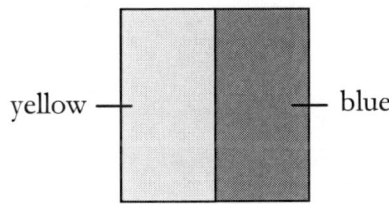

1. Cut a 2" x 3½" rectangle each of yellow and blue.
2. Lay out pieces as shown and sew together.
3. Press.

Letter L - traditionally pieced

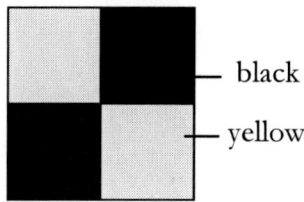

1. Cut 2, 2" x 2" yellow squares.
2. Cut 2, 2" x 2" black squares.
3. Lay out squares as shown.
4. Sew together in 2 rows of 2 squares.
5. Sew together rows carefully matching seams at centre.
6. Press.

Letter M - foundation pieced

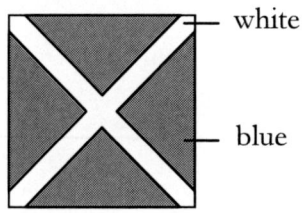

1. Copy templates for Unit A and Unit B.
2. Piece Unit A and Unit B using blue and white.
3. Join Units together taking care to visually align diagonal seams.
4. Trim to an accurate 3½" x 3½" square.

Letter N - traditionally pieced

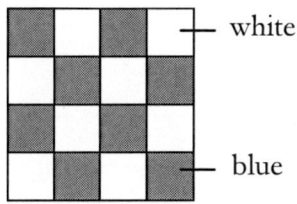

1. Cut 8, 1¼" x 1¼" blue squares.
2. Cut 8, 1¼" x 1¼" white squares.
3. Lay out squares as shown.
4. Sew together in 4 rows of 4 squares.
5. Sew together rows carefully matching seams at intersections.
6. Press.

Letter O - traditionally pieced, makes 2 blocks

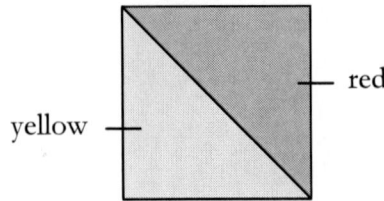

1. Cut a 4" x 4" square each of red and yellow.
2. Place right sides together. Draw a diagonal line across the back of the yellow square.
3. Stitch each side of the line and then cut along the drawn line.
4. Open out and press allowance towards red side.
5. Trim blocks to an accurate 3½" x 3½" square.

Letter P - traditionally pieced

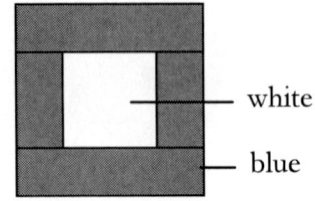

1. Cut 2, 3½" x 1¼" blue rectangles.
2. Cut 2, 1¼" x 2" blue rectangles.
3. Cut a 2" x 2" white square.
4. Lay out pieces as shown.
5. Join middle section first and then add blue rectangles.
6. Press.

Letter Q

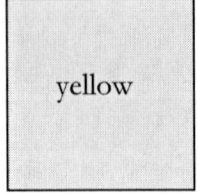

Cut 1, 3½" x 3½" yellow square.

Letter R - traditionally pieced

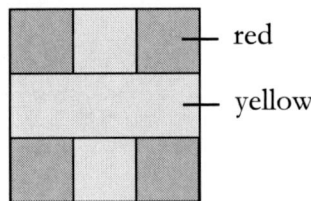

1. Cut 4, 1½" x 1½" red squares.
2. Cut 2, 1½" x 1½" yellow squares.
3. Cut a 3½" x 1½" yellow rectangle.
4. Lay out pieces as shown.
5. Sew together the 2 rows of 3 squares.
6. Sew together rows taking care to visually align vertical seams.
7. Press.

Letter S - traditionally pieced

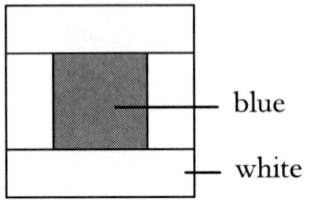

1. Cut 2, 3½" x 1¼" white rectangles.
2. Cut 2, 1¼" x 2" white rectangles.
3. Cut a 2" x 2" blue square.
4. Lay out pieces as shown.
5. Join middle section first and then add white rectangles.
6. Press.

Letter T - traditionally pieced

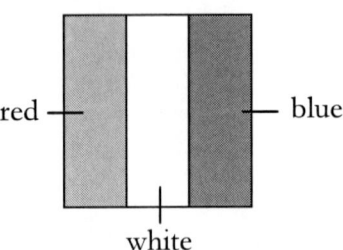

1. Cut a 1½" x 3½" rectangle each of red, white and blue.
2. Lay out pieces as shown and sew together.
3. Press.

Letter U - traditionally pieced

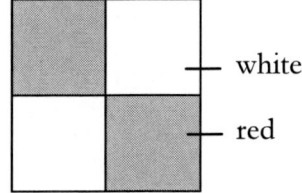

1. Cut 2, 2" x 2" red squares.
2. Cut 2, 2" x 2" white squares.
3. Lay out squares as shown.
4. Sew together in 2 rows of 2 squares.
5. Sew together rows carefully matching seams at centre.
6. Press.

Letter V - foundation pieced

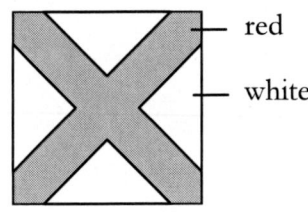

1. Copy template for Units A and B.
2. Piece both Units using red and white.
3. Join Units together taking care to visually align diagonal seams.
4. Trim to an accurate 3½" x 3½" square.
5. Remove papers.

Letter W - foundation pieced

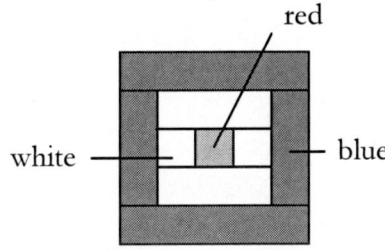

1. Copy block template.
2. Piece block using red, white and blue.
3. Trim to an accurate 3½" x 3½" square.
4. Remove papers.

Letter X - traditionally pieced

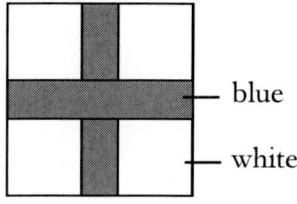

1. Cut 4, 1¾" x 1¾" white squares.
2. Cut 2, 1" x 1¾" blue rectangles.
3. Cut a 3½" x 1" blue rectangle.
4. Lay out pieces as shown.
5. Sew together the 2 rows of 2 squares and rectangle.
6. Sew together rows taking care to visually align vertical seams.
7. Press.

Letter Y - foundation pieced

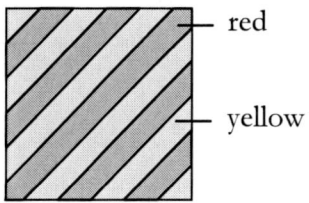

1. Copy block template.
2. Piece block using red and yellow fabrics.
3. Trim to an accurate 3½" x 3½" square.
4. Remove papers.

Letter Z - foundation pieced

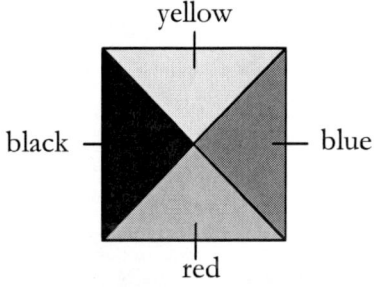

1. Copy block template.
2. Piece Unit A using yellow and black.
3. Piece Unit B using red and blue.
4. Join Units together carefully matching centres.
5. Trim to an accurate 3½" x 3½" square.
6. Remove papers.

BASIC BLOCK
Foundation Papers
(reversed ready for piecing)

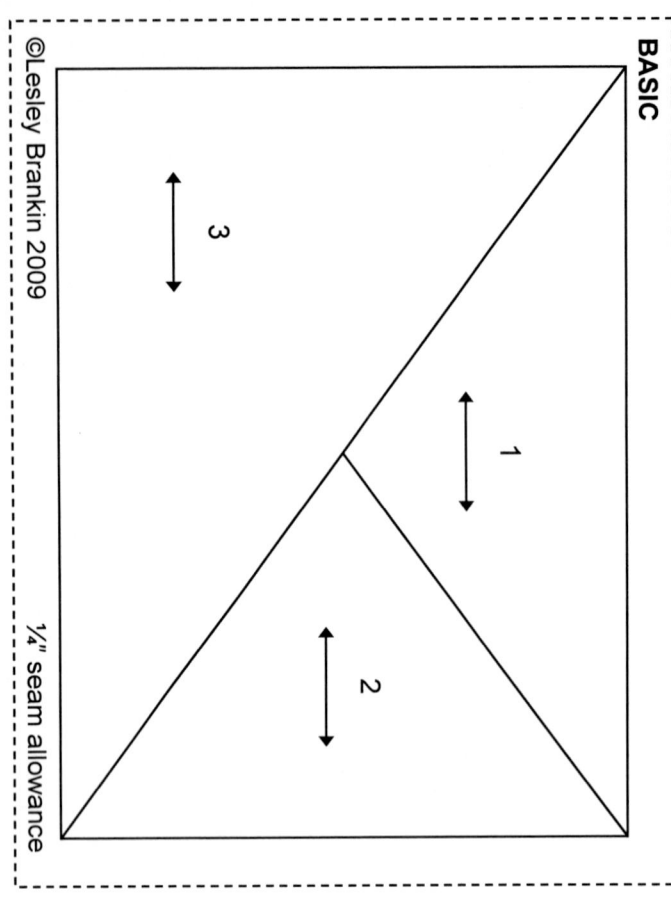

Fabric Key

Refer to relevant section instructions for details of which fabrics to use.

Align stripes in this direction if appropriate

Finished Block Size: 4" wide x 3" high

Kindly respect my copyright and only make copies for your personal use

Second Identical Copy - saving paper

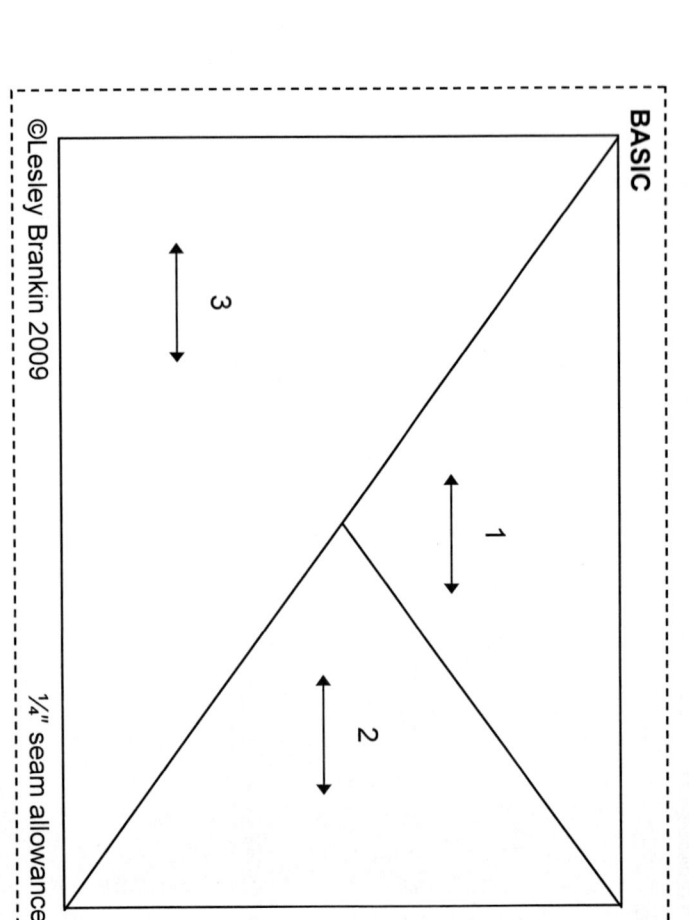

28

BASIC BLOCKS REVERSED & HALF DIAGONAL

Foundation Papers
(reversed ready for piecing)

BASIC - Half Diagonal

1

2

Use this line for reversed diagonal

¼" seam allowance

©Lesley Brankin 2009

Kindly respect my copyright and only make copies for your personal use

BASIC - Reversed

1

2

3

¼" seam allowance

©Lesley Brankin 2009

Fabric Key

Refer to relevant section instructions for details of which fabrics to use.

Align stripes in this direction if appropriate

Finished Block Size: 4" wide x 3" high

29

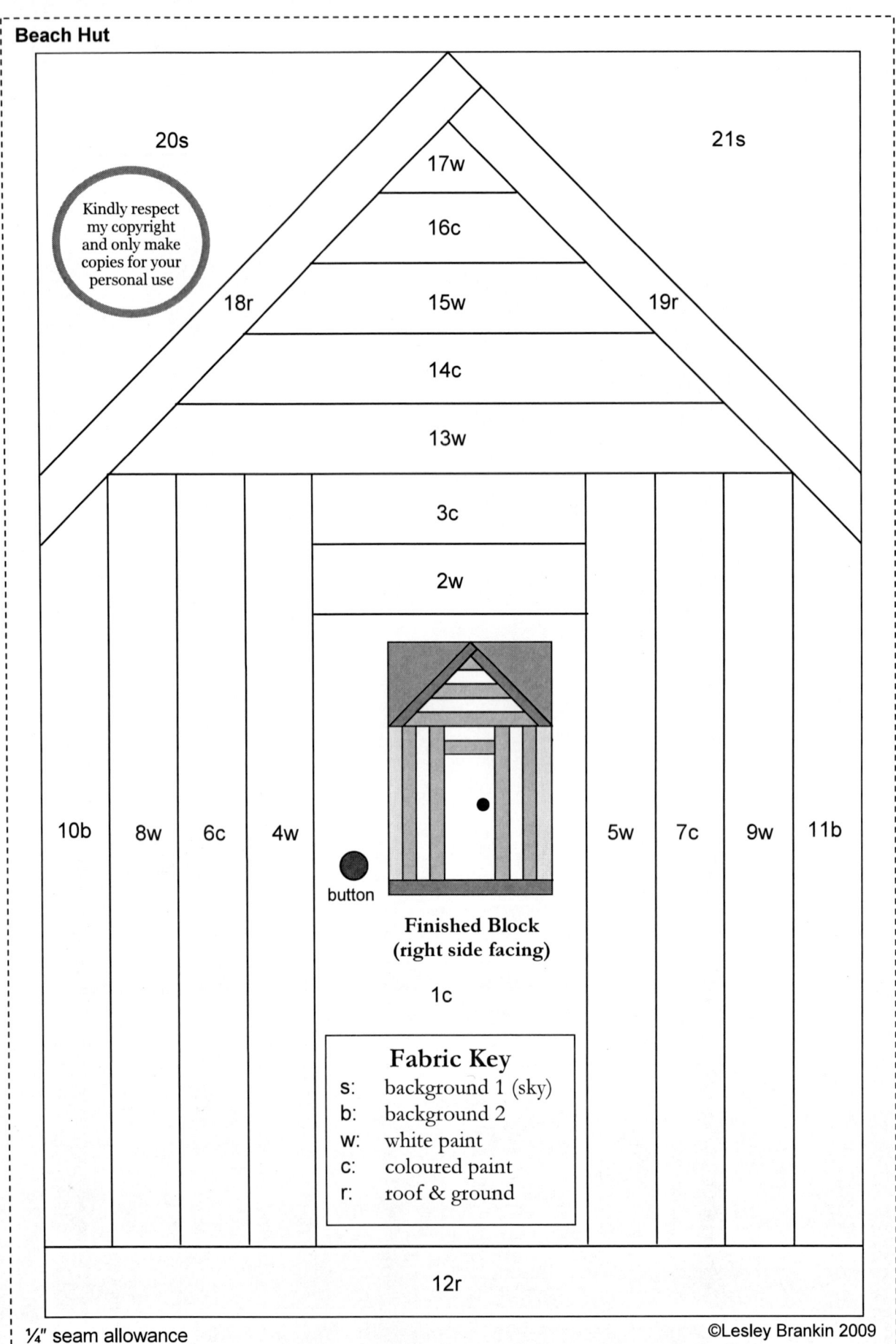

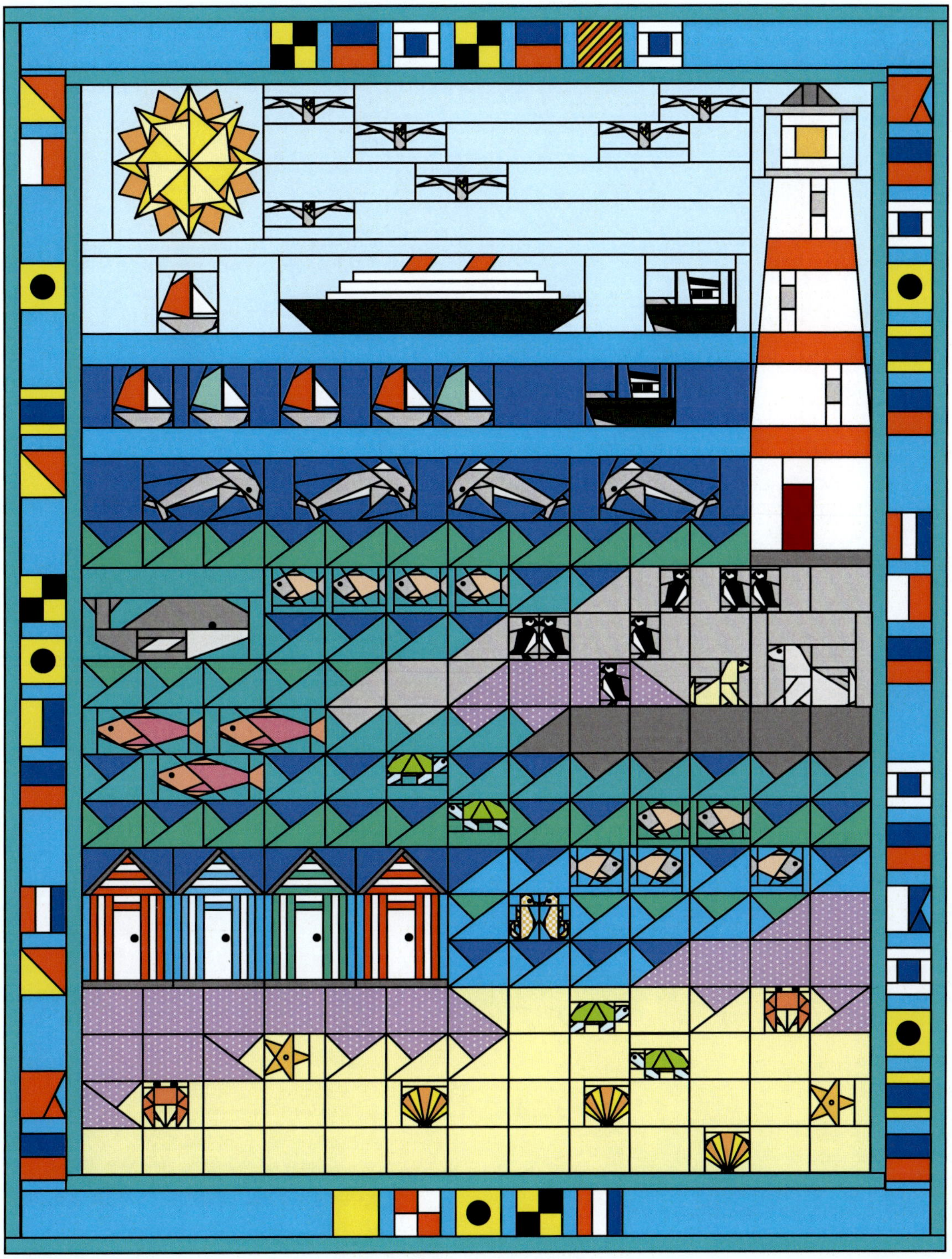

General Layout Diagram

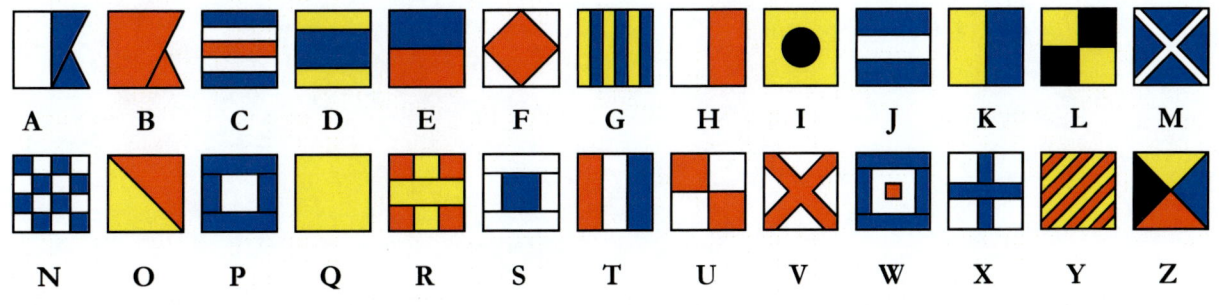

Nautical Flag Blocks

Clam Shell

Crab

At the Beach . . .

Starfish

Turtle

Beach Hut

& In the Sea . . .

Seahorses

Kindly Note
that images are not to relative scale

Large Fish

32

In & On the Sea . . .

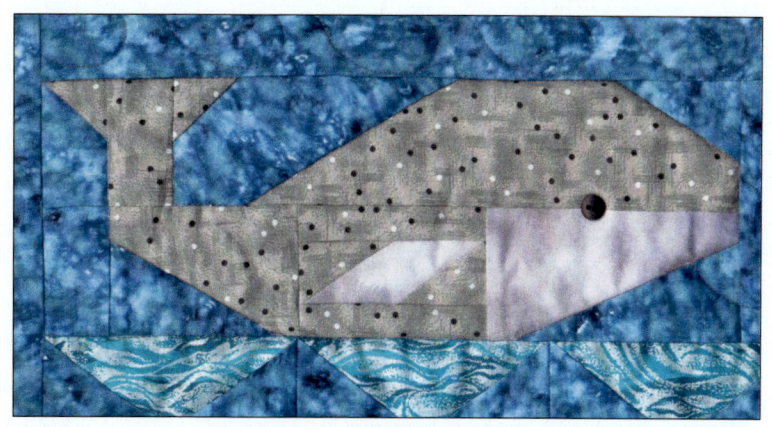
Whale

Small Fish

Dolphin

Yacht

Trawler

Cruise Liner

Lighthouse

Sun

Seagull

In the Sky & On Land…

Puffins

Baby & Mother Seal

Kindly Note that images are not to relative scale

34

CRAB BLOCK

Foundation Papers
(reversed ready for piecing)

Fabric Key
- s: sand
- b: body

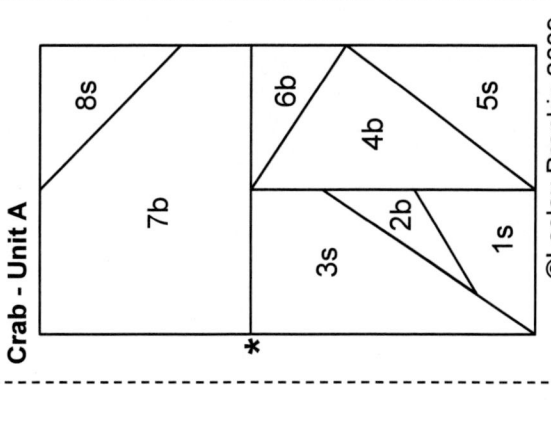

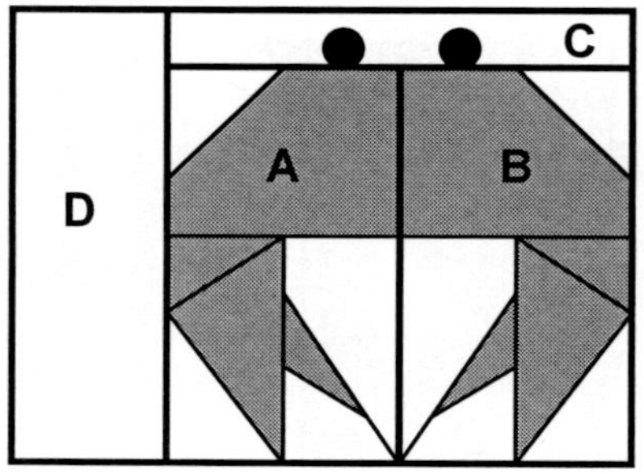

©Lesley Brankin 2009

¼" seam allowance

Add the following strips to Unit A+B:

UNIT C: 3½" x ⅞" (at top of crab)
UNIT D: 1½" x 3½" (to either side of crab)

Finished Block Size: 4" wide x 3" high

CLAM SHELL BLOCK

Foundation Papers
(reversed ready for piecing)

Fabric Key
- s: sand
- b: shell
- c: contrast shell

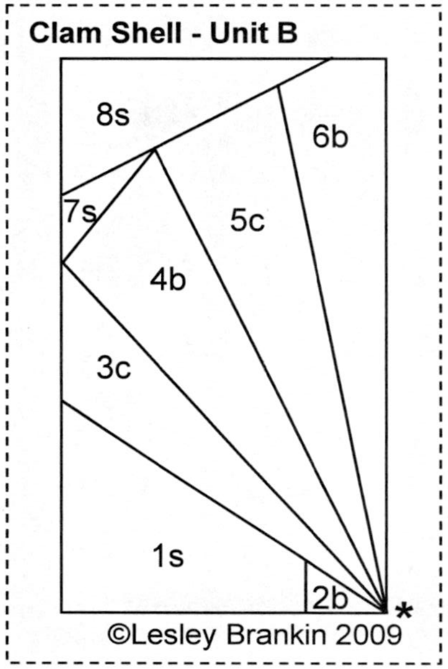

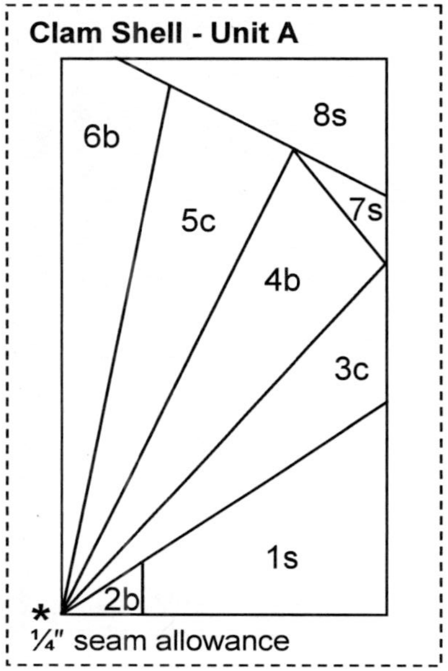

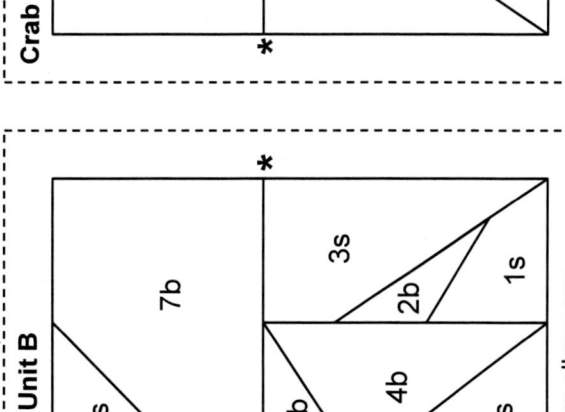

©Lesley Brankin 2009

¼" seam allowance

Kindly respect my copyright and only make copies for your personal use

* match when joining units

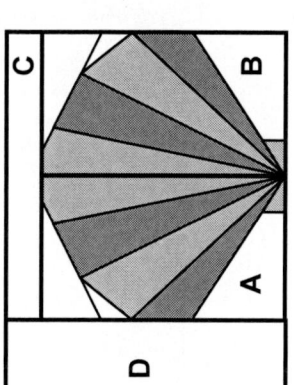

Finished Blocks
(right side facing)

Add the following strips to Unit A+B:

UNIT C: 3½" x ⅞" (at top of shell)
UNIT D: 1½" x 3½" (to either side of shell)

Finished Block Size: 4" wide x 3" high

35

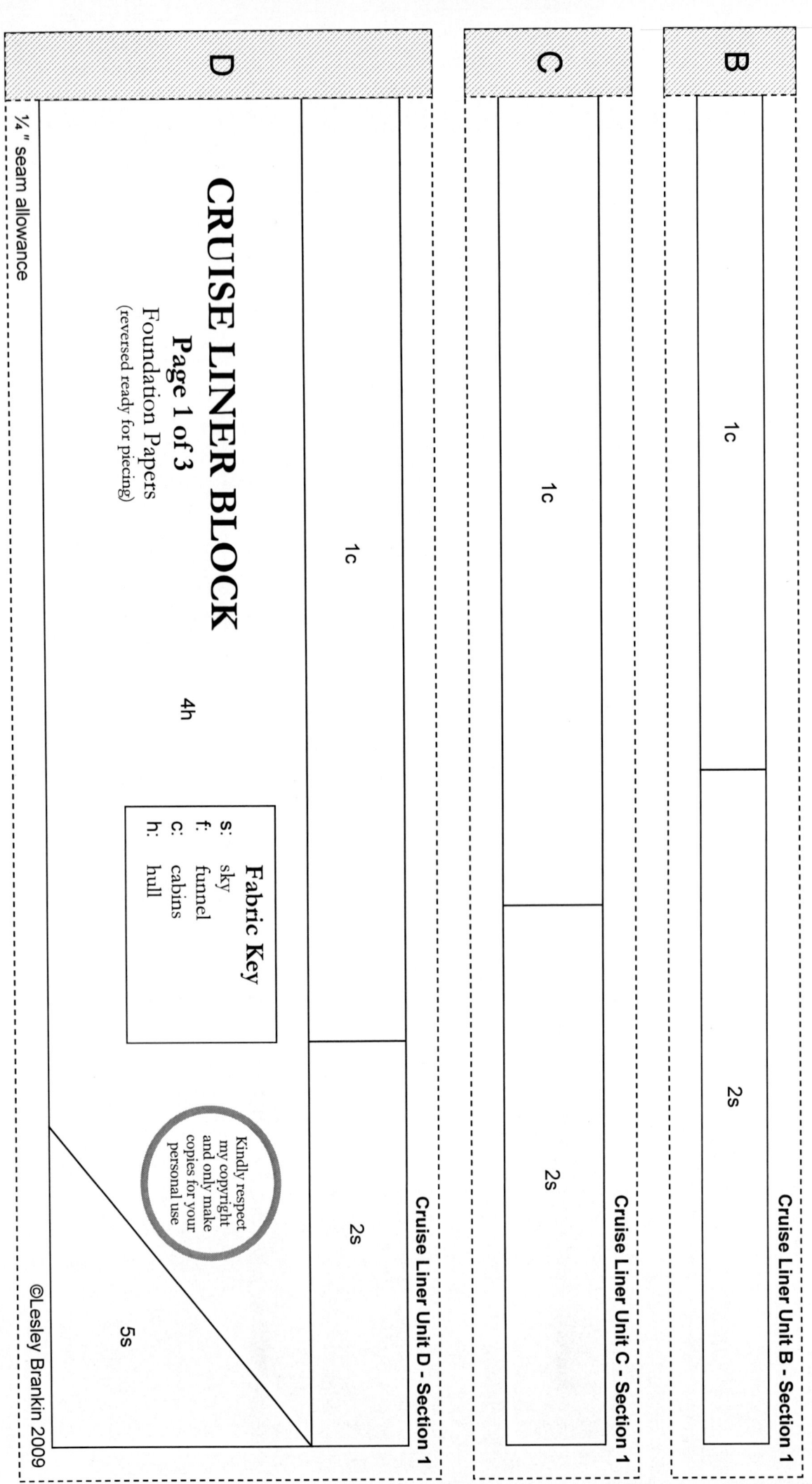

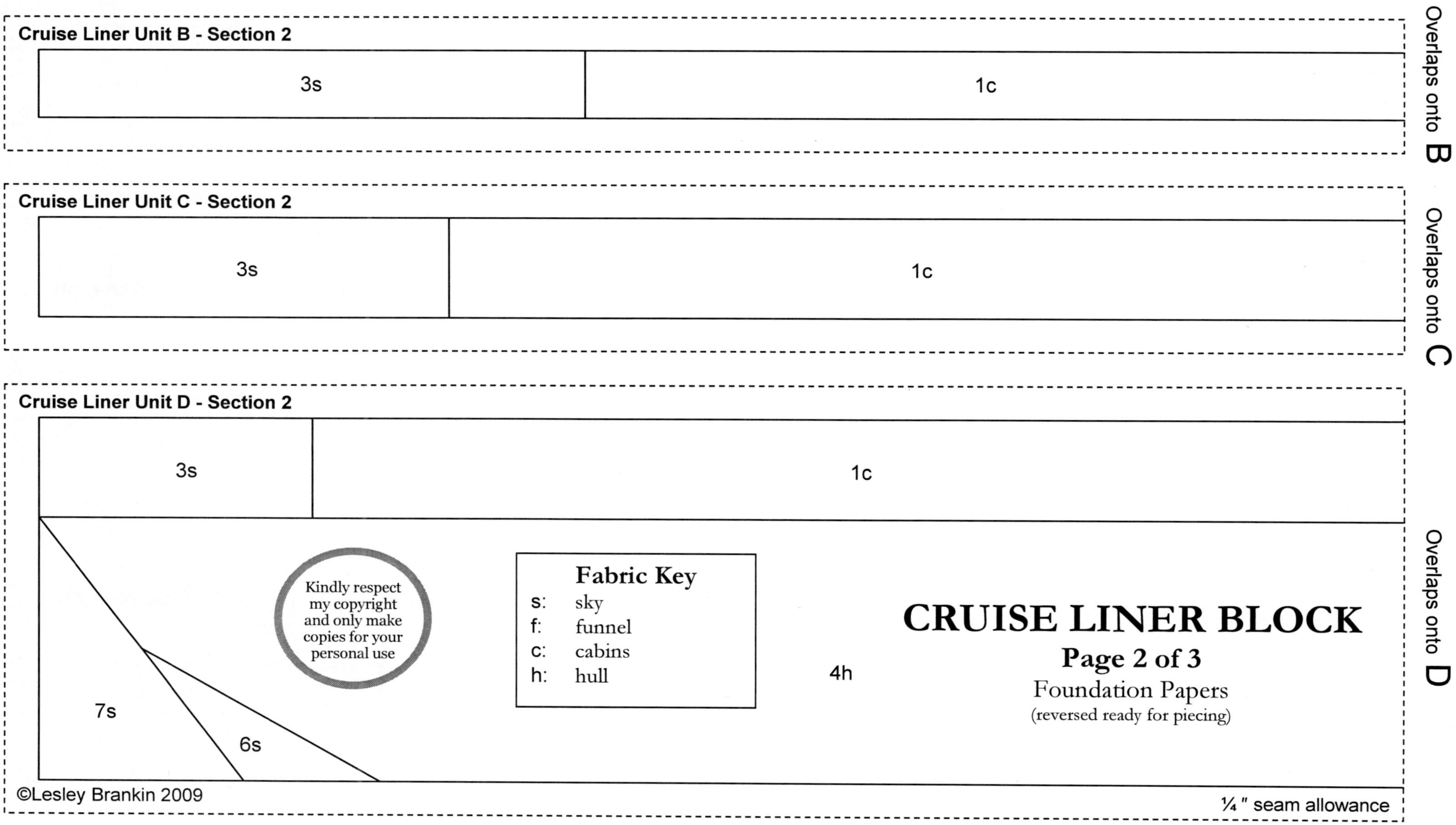

Overlaps onto **B**   Overlaps onto **C**   Overlaps onto **D**

CRUISE LINER BLOCK
Page 2 of 3
Foundation Papers
(reversed ready for piecing)

1c

1c

1c

4h

Fabric Key
s: sky
f: funnel
c: cabins
h: hull

Kindly respect my copyright and only make copies for your personal use

3s

3s

3s

6s

7s

Cruise Liner Unit B - Section 2

Cruise Liner Unit C - Section 2

Cruise Liner Unit D - Section 2

©Lesley Brankin 2009

¼" seam allowance

CRUISE LINER BLOCK
Page 3 of 3
Foundation Papers
(reversed ready for piecing)

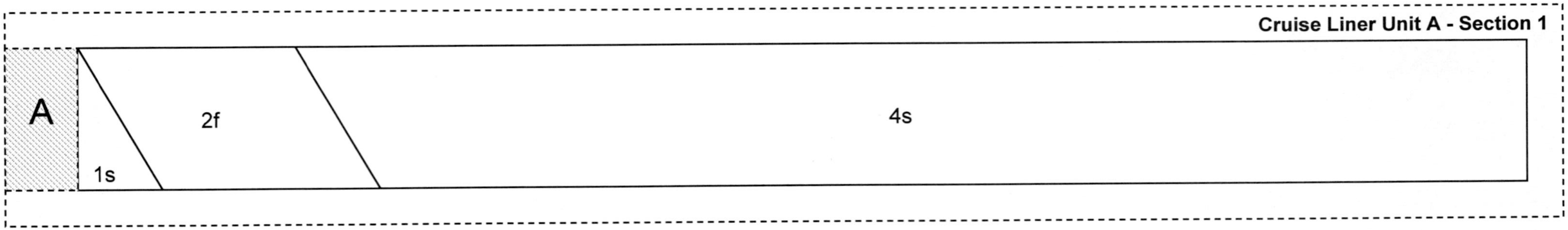

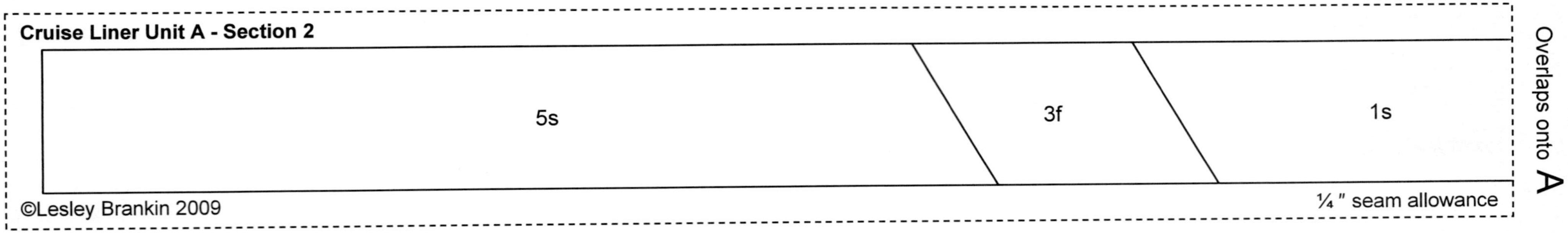

Cruise Liner Unit A - Section 1

A

1s

2f

Cruise Liner Unit A - Section 2

5s

4s

3f

1s

Overlaps onto A

¼" seam allowance

©Lesley Brankin 2009

Kindly respect my copyright and only make copies for your personal use

Fabric Key
- s: sky
- f: funnel
- c: cabin/upper decks
- h: hull

Finished Block Size: 20" wide x 5" high

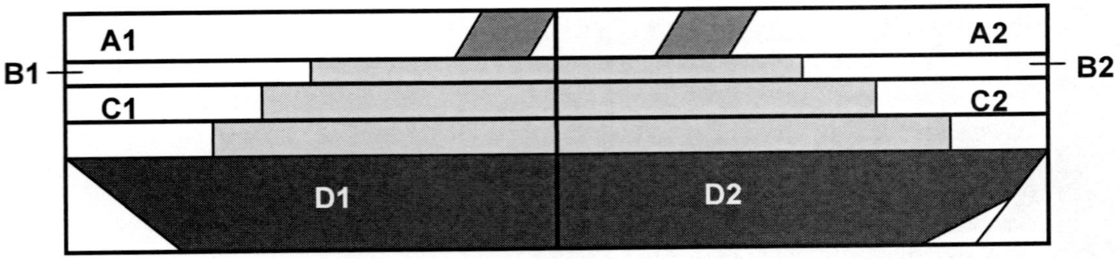

Finished Block (right side facing)

A1, B1, C1, D1, A2, B2, C2, D2

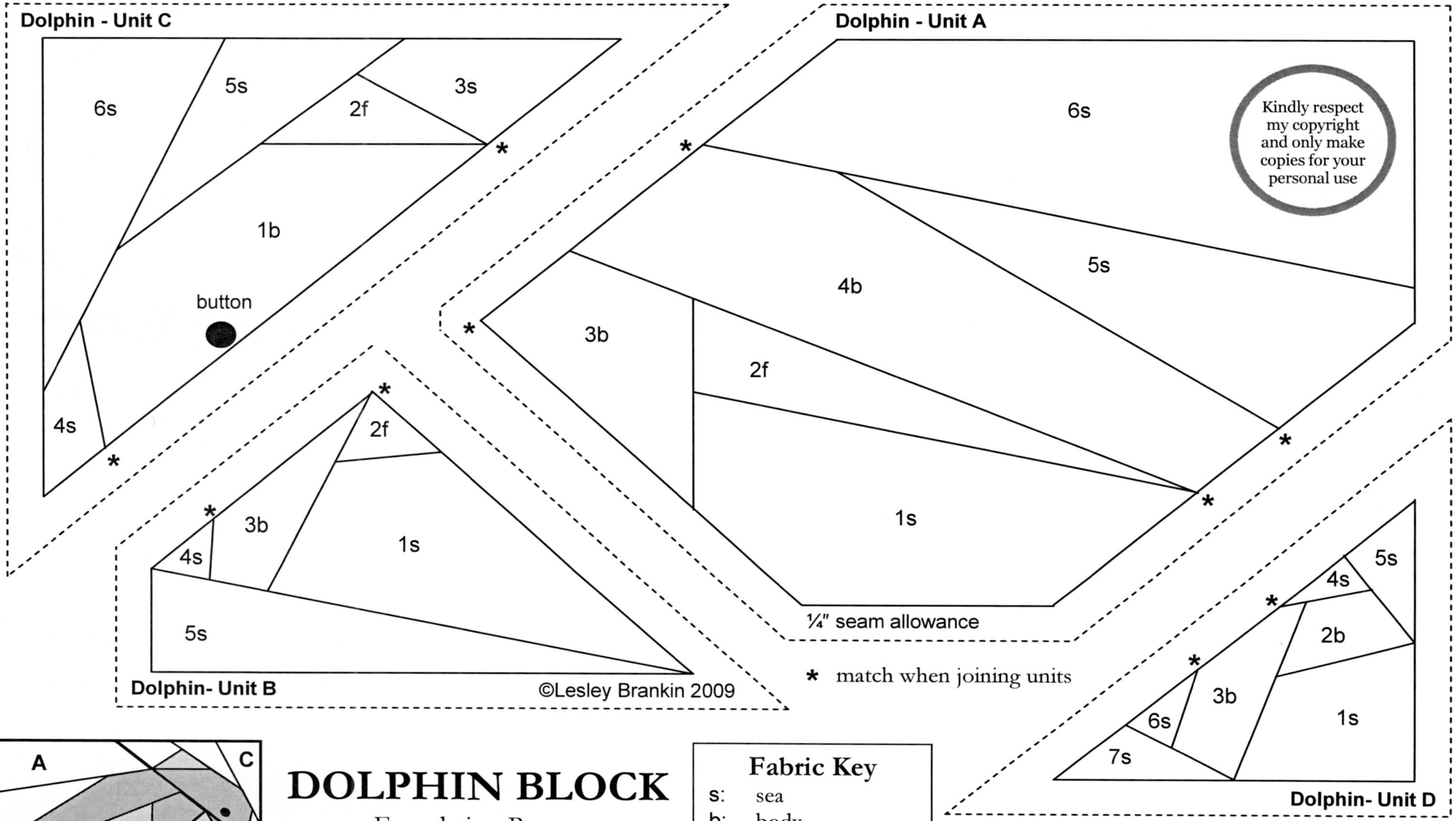

DOLPHIN BLOCK

Foundation Papers
(reversed ready for piecing)

©Lesley Brankin 2009

Dolphin - Unit A
- 6s
- 5s
- 4b
- 2f
- 1s
- 3b

Kindly respect my copyright and only make copies for your personal use

Dolphin - Unit B
- 1s
- 2f
- 3b
- 4s
- 5s

Dolphin - Unit C
- 6s
- 5s
- 3s
- 2f
- 1b (button)
- 4s

Dolphin - Unit D
- 5s
- 4s
- 2b
- 1s
- 3b
- 6s
- 7s

¼" seam allowance

* match when joining units

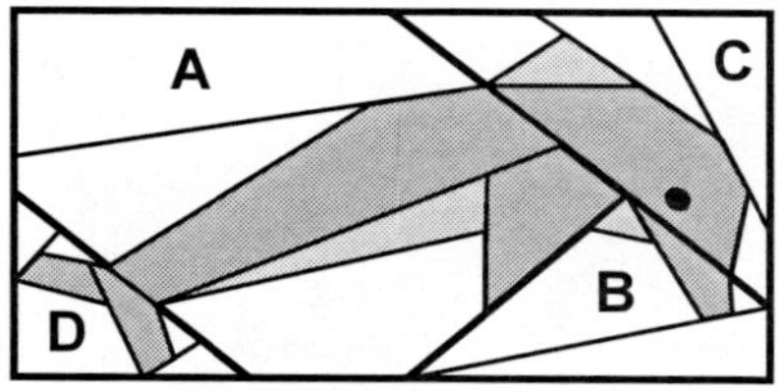

Fabric Key
- s: sea
- b: body
- f: fin, under belly

Finished Block Size: 8" wide × 4" high

Finished Block
(right side facing)

A, B, C, D

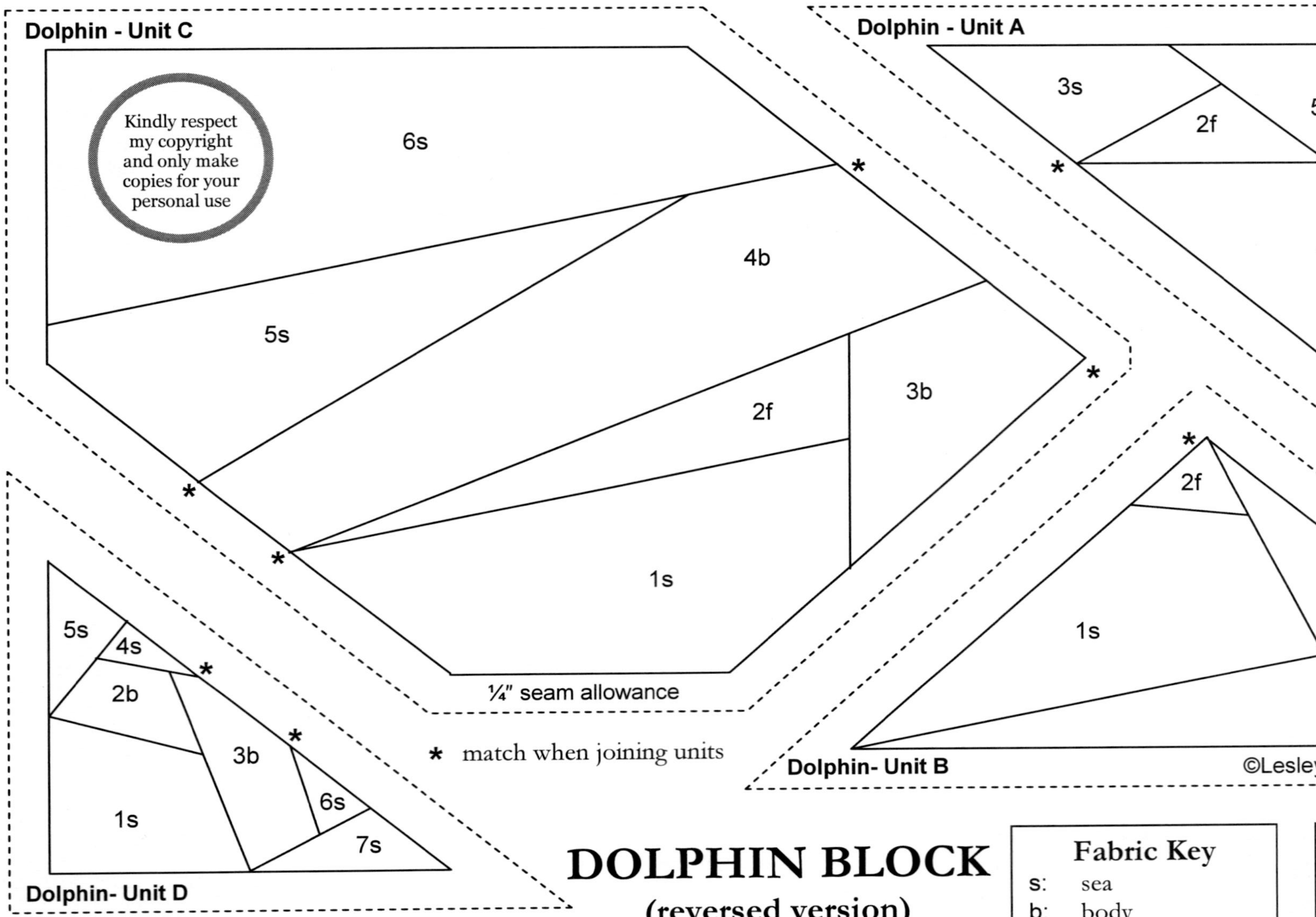

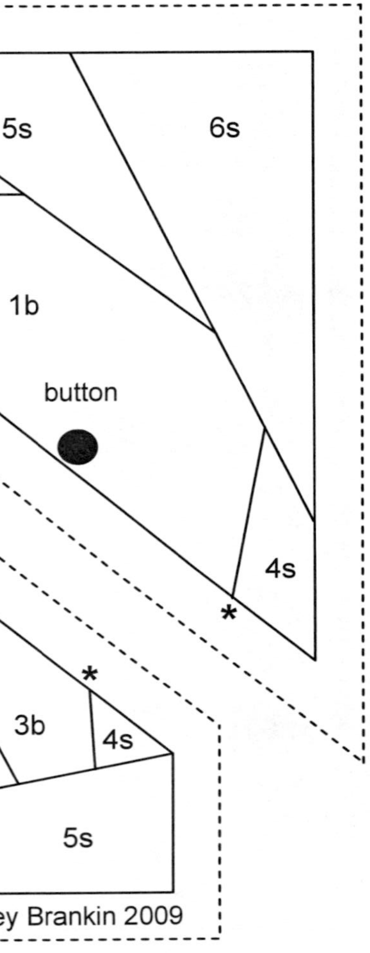

DOLPHIN BLOCK (reversed version)

Foundation Papers
(reversed ready for piecing)

Kindly respect my copyright and only make copies for your personal use

Dolphin - Unit A
Dolphin - Unit B
Dolphin - Unit C
Dolphin - Unit D

* match when joining units

¼" seam allowance

button

©Lesley Brankin 2009

Fabric Key
- s: sea
- b: body
- c: contrast

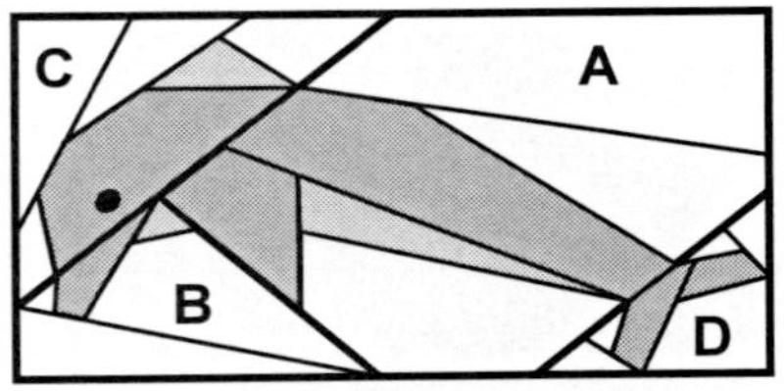

Finished Block Size: 8" wide x 4" high

Finished Block
(right side facing)

FISH - LARGE BLOCK

Foundation Papers
(reversed ready for piecing)

* match when joining units

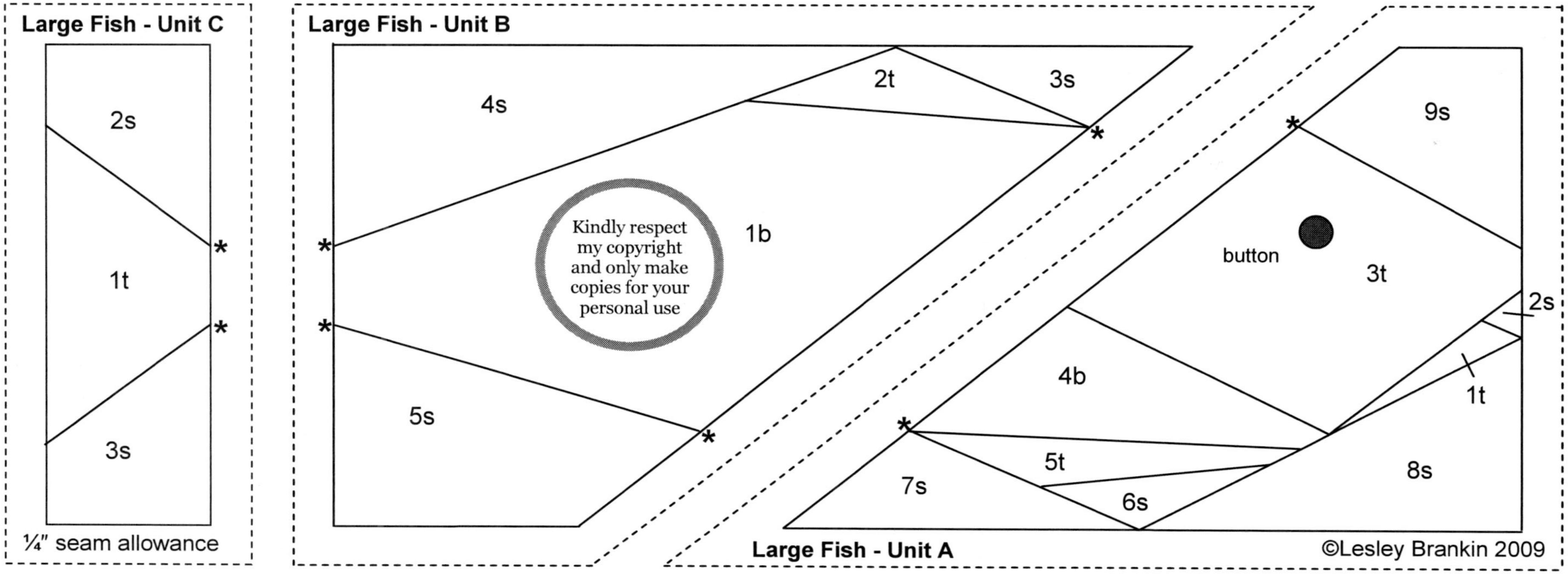

Large Fish - Unit A

9s, 2s, 1t, 3t (button), 8s, 6s, 5t, 4b, 7s, 3s, 2t

©Lesley Brankin 2009

Large Fish - Unit B

4s, 1b (Kindly respect my copyright and only make copies for your personal use), 5s

Large Fish - Unit C

2s, 1t, 3s

¼" seam allowance

Add the following strip to Unit A+B+C:

UNIT D: 1½" x 3½" (to either left or right of fish)

Finished Block Size: 8" wide x 3" high

Fabric Key

b: body
t: tail, fin, head
s: sea

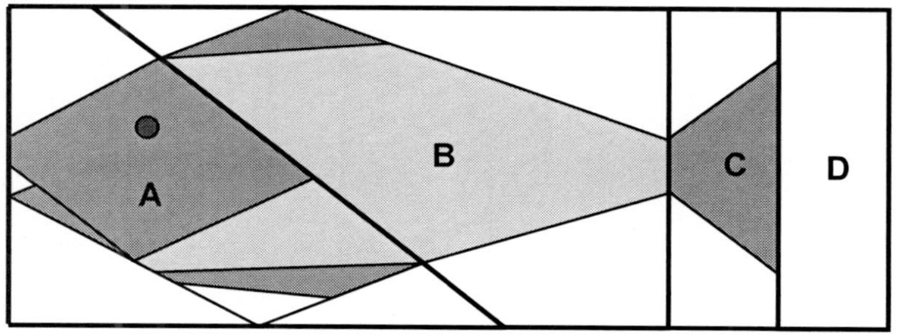

Finished Block
(right side facing)

FISH - SMALL BLOCK
Foundation Papers

Fabric Key
b: body
t: tail, fin, face
s: sea

Add the following strips to Unit A+B+C:

UNIT D: 3½" x 1" (to either top or bottom of fish)
UNIT E: 1" x 3½" (to either left or right of fish)

Finished Block Size: 4" wide x 3" high

* match when joining units

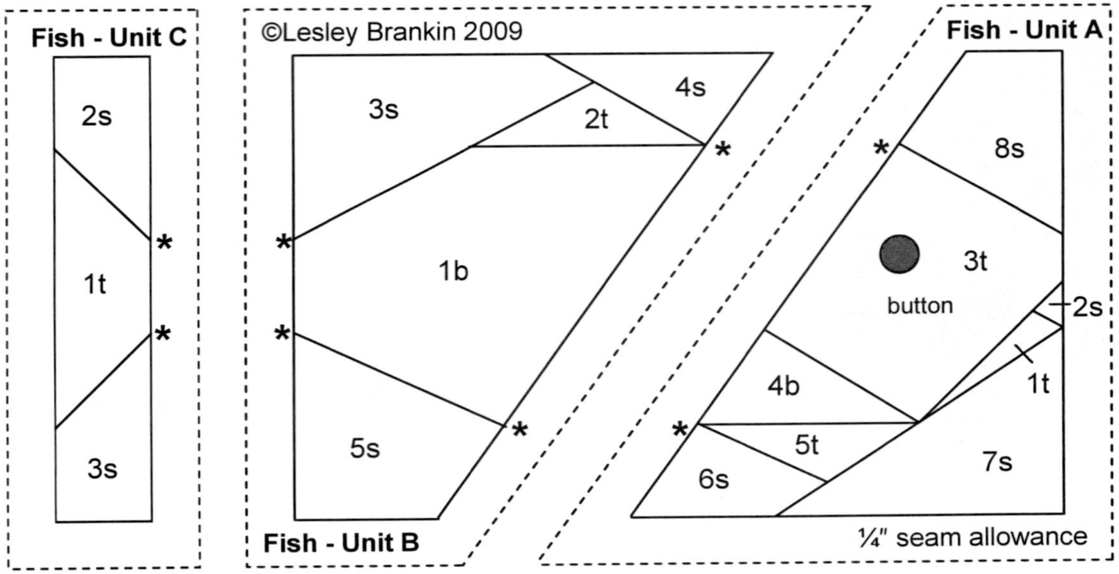

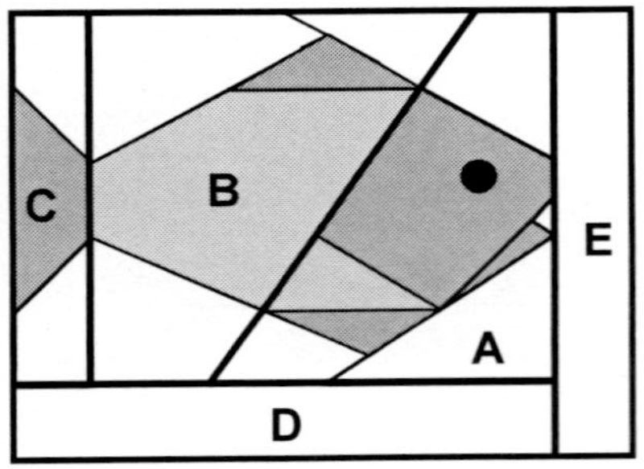

Finished Block (right side facing)

¼" seam allowance

Fish - Unit A
Fish - Unit B
Fish - Unit C

©Lesley Brankin 2009

Kindly respect my copyright and only make copies for your personal use

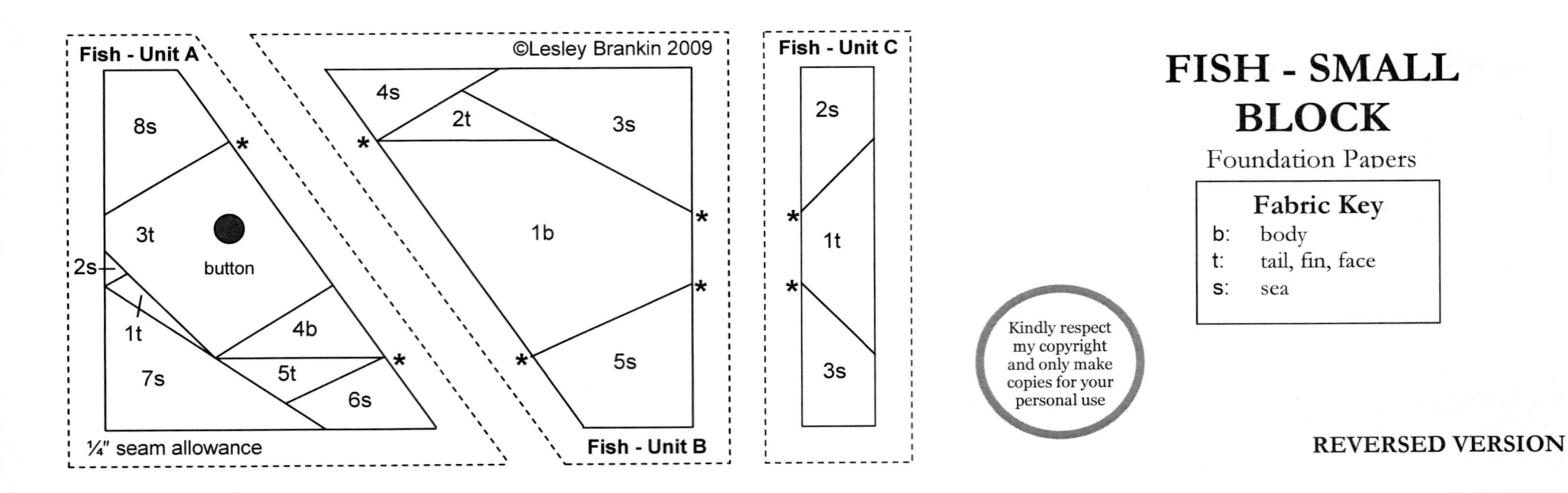

REVERSED VERSION

Fish - Unit A
Fish - Unit B
Fish - Unit C

Lighthouse - Unit B

This block is made up from 9 Units A through I

H G F E D C B A I

Finished Block
(right side facing)

LIGHTHOUSE BLOCK
Page 1 of 5
Foundation Papers
(reversed ready for piecing)

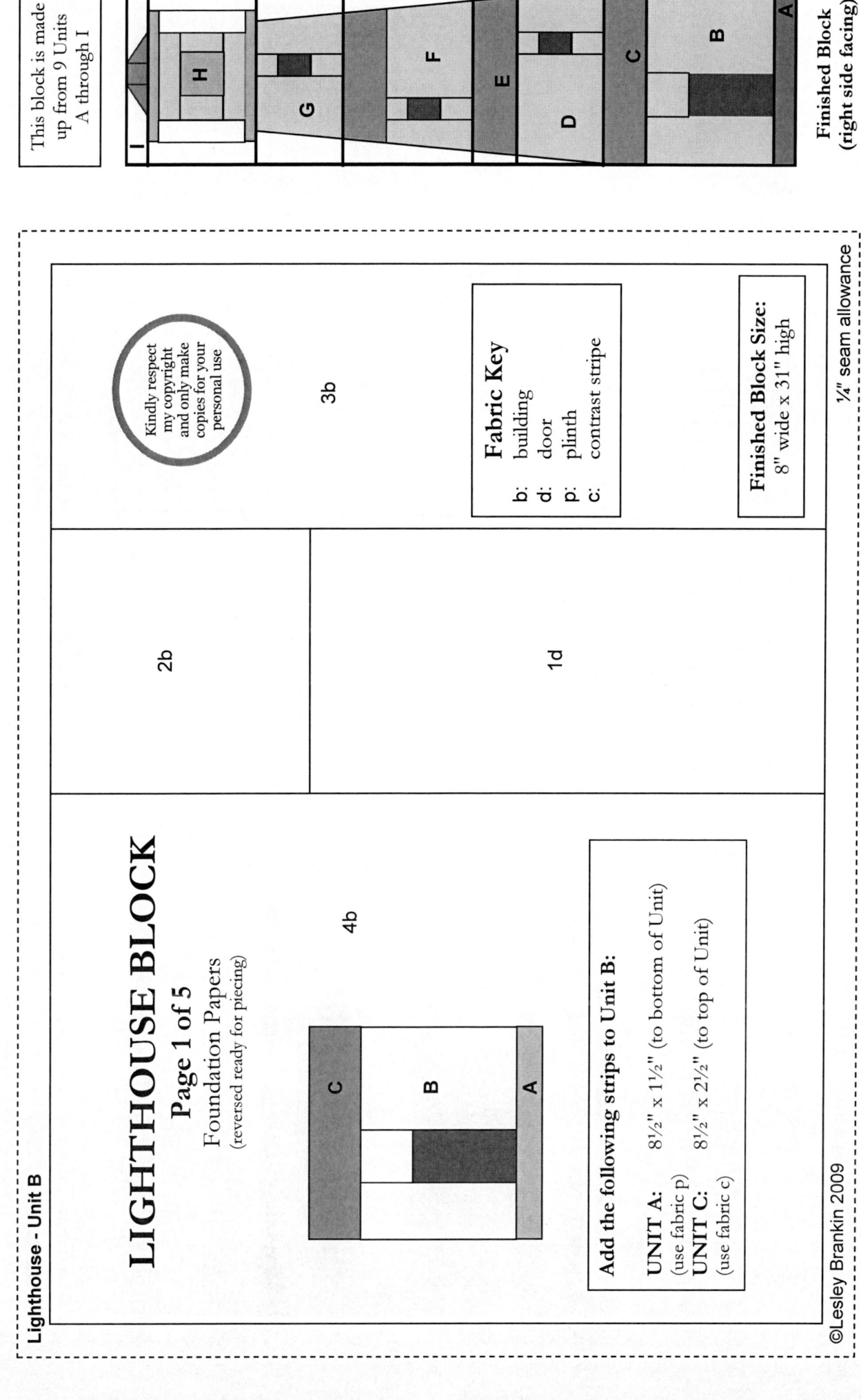

2b

1d

3b

4b

Fabric Key
b: building
d: door
p: plinth
c: contrast stripe

Finished Block Size:
8" wide x 31" high

¼" seam allowance

Kindly respect my copyright and only make copies for your personal use

Add the following strips to Unit B:

UNIT A: 8½" x 1½" (to bottom of Unit)
(use fabric p)
UNIT C: 8½" x 2½" (to top of Unit)
(use fabric c)

©Lesley Brankin 2009

43

LIGHTHOUSE BLOCK
Page 2 of 5
Foundation Papers
(reversed ready for piecing)

©Lesley Brankin 2009

Kindly respect my copyright and only make copies for your personal use

Lighthouse - Unit E

2a

1c

3a

Lighthouse - Unit D

6s

4b

2b | 1w | 3b

5b

7s

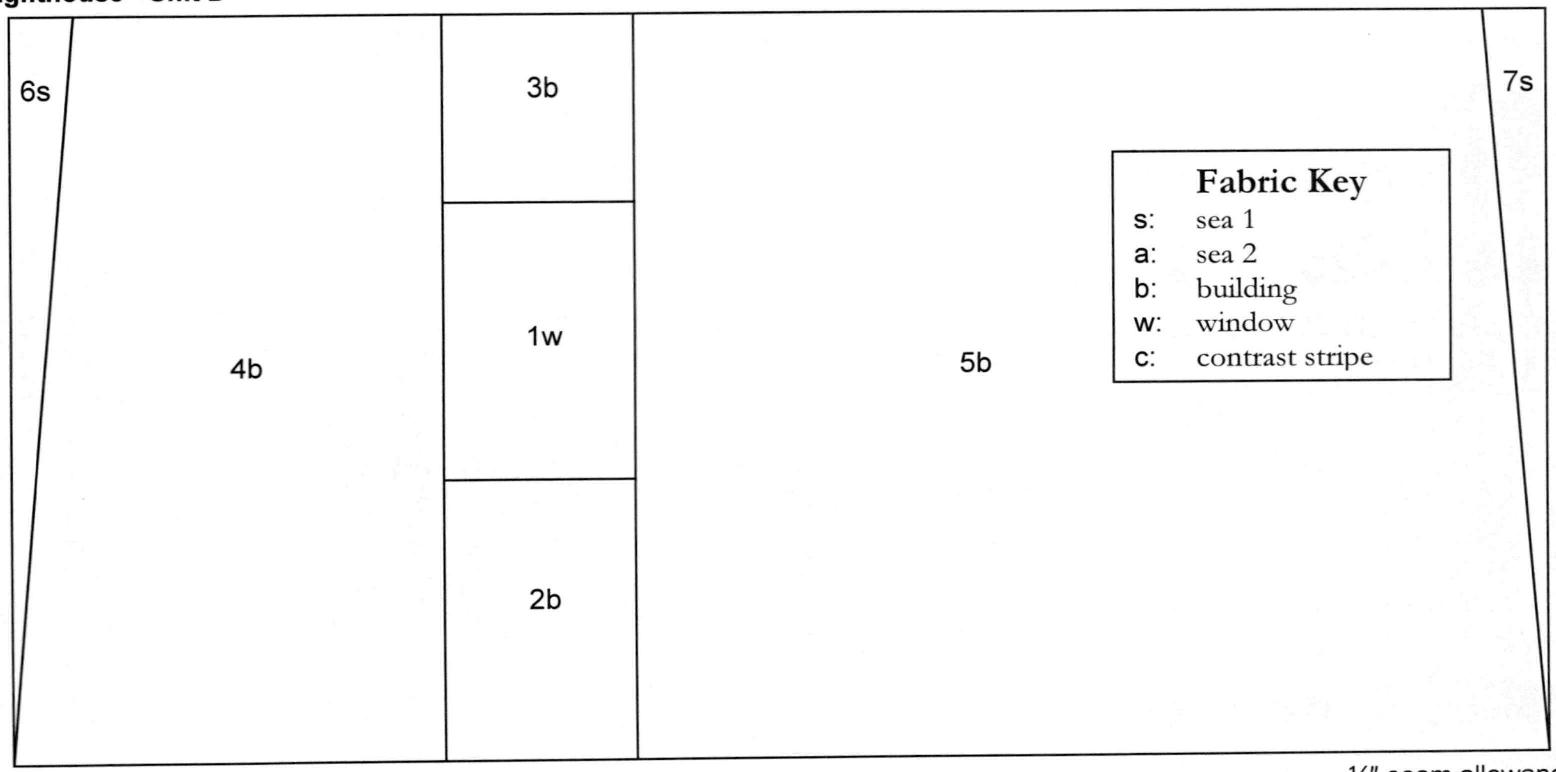

Fabric Key

s: sea 1
a: sea 2
b: building
w: window
c: contrast stripe

¼" seam allowance

44

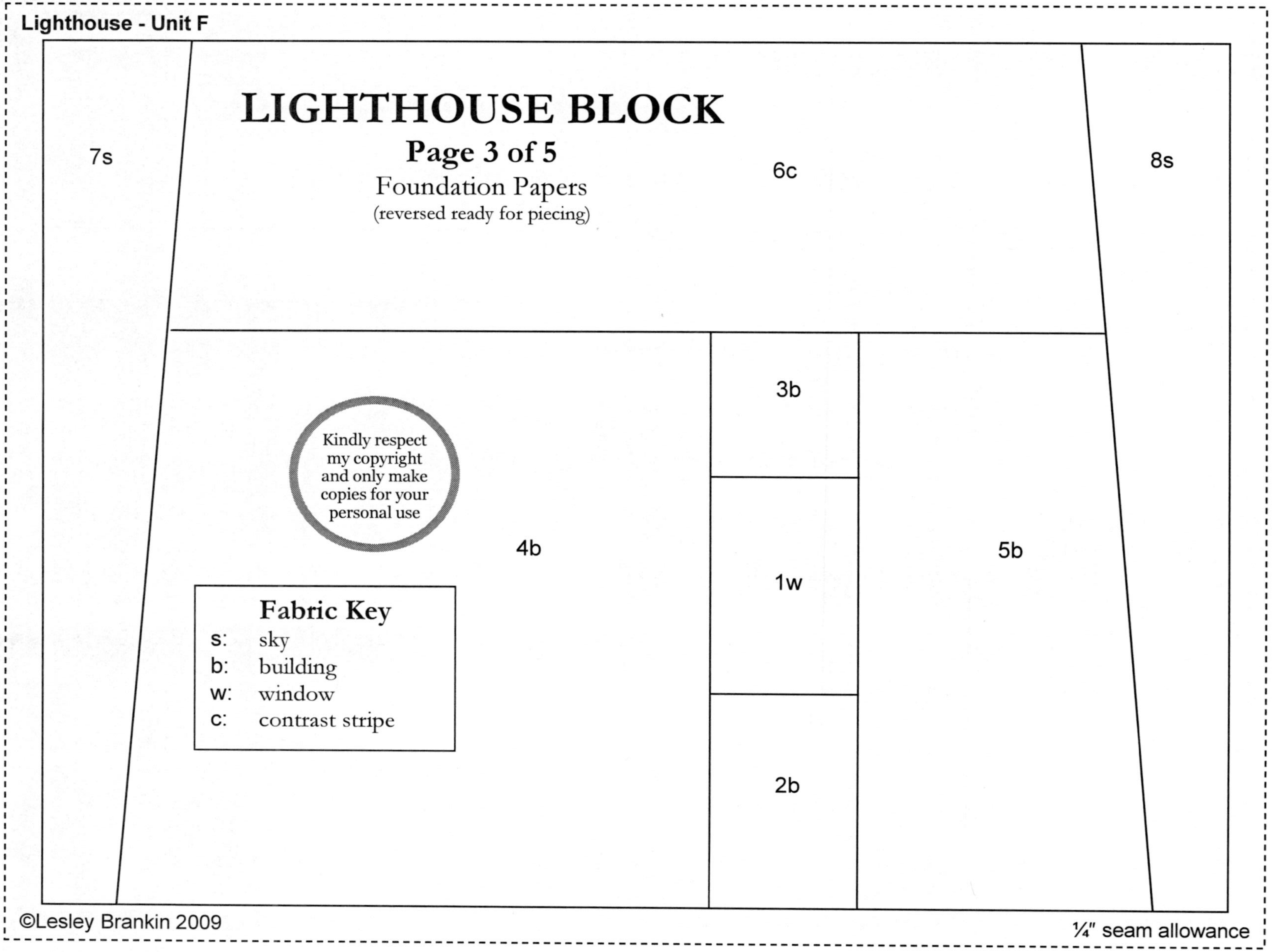

Lighthouse - Unit F

LIGHTHOUSE BLOCK
Page 3 of 5
Foundation Papers
(reversed ready for piecing)

¼" seam allowance

8s

5b

6c

3b | 1w | 2b

4b

Kindly respect my copyright and only make copies for your personal use

Fabric Key
s: sky
b: building
w: window
c: contrast stripe

7s

©Lesley Brankin 2009

Lighthouse - Unit I

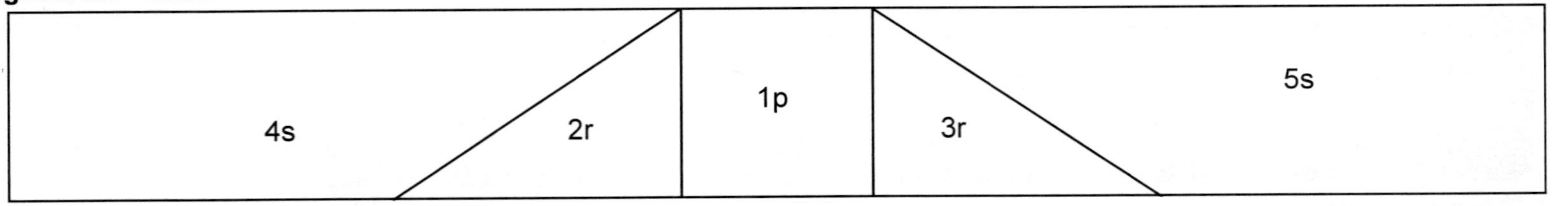

©Lesley Brankin 2009

4s

2r

1p

3r

5s

¼" seam allowance

Lighthouse - Unit G

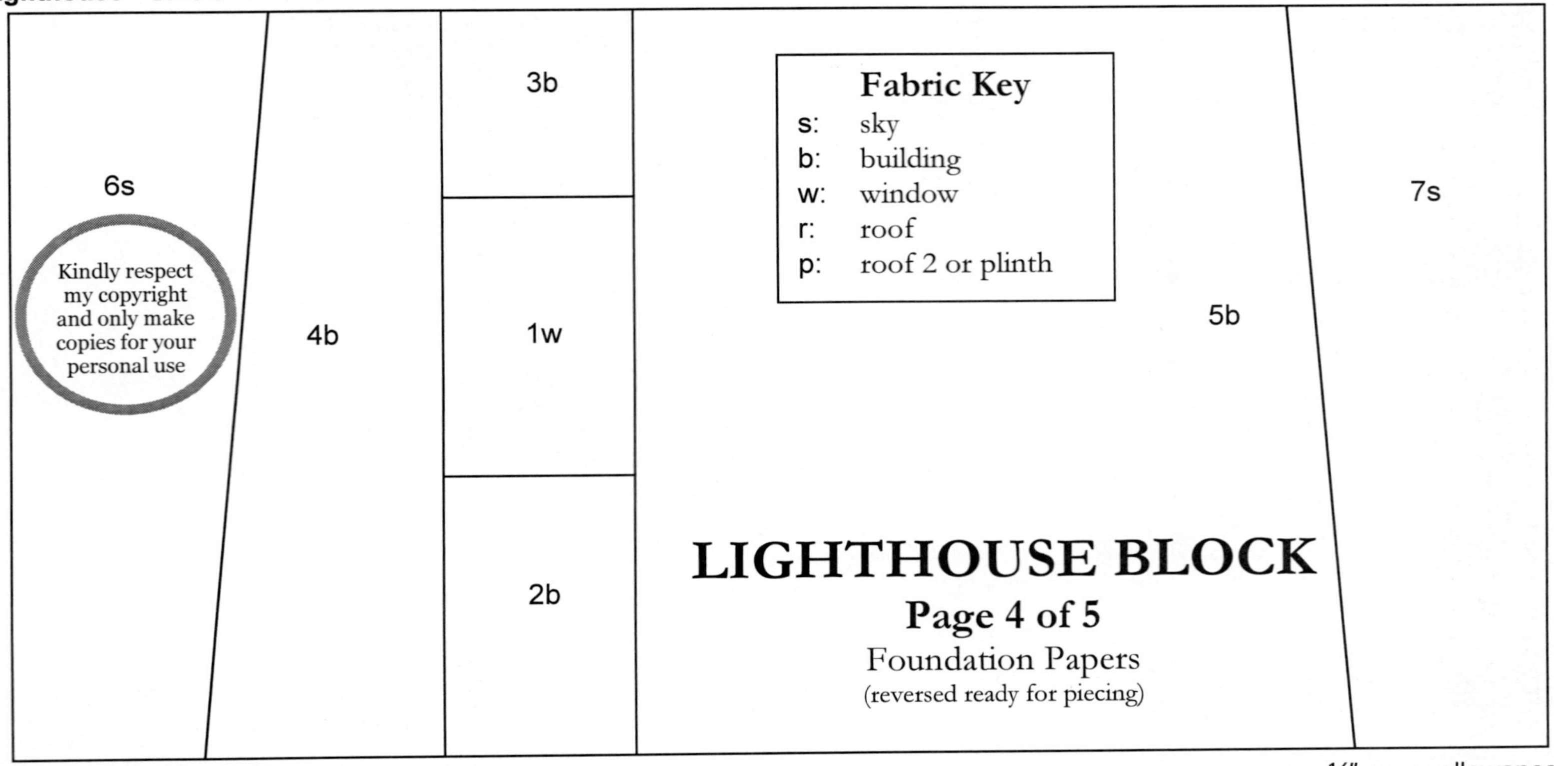

©Lesley Brankin 2009

Kindly respect my copyright and only make copies for your personal use

6s

4b

3b

1w

2b

Fabric Key

s: sky
b: building
w: window
r: roof
p: roof 2 or plinth

LIGHTHOUSE BLOCK
Page 4 of 5
Foundation Papers
(reversed ready for piecing)

5b

7s

¼" seam allowance

LIGHTHOUSE BLOCK - Page 5 of 5

Foundation Papers
(reversed ready for piecing)

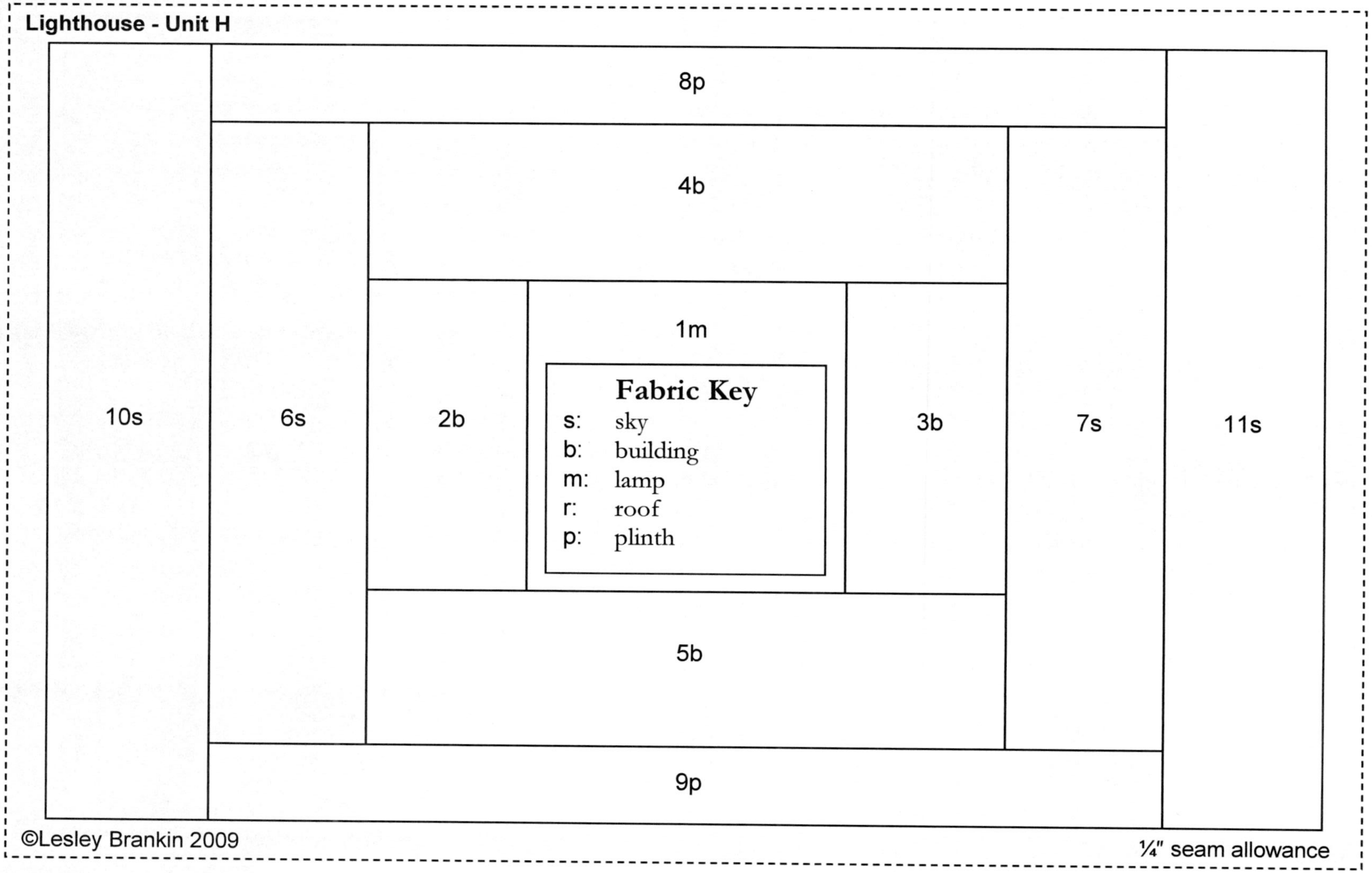

Kindly respect my copyright and only make copies for your personal use

Lighthouse - Unit H

11s

7s

3b

8p

4b

1m

Fabric Key

s: sky
b: building
m: lamp
r: roof
p: plinth

2b

5b

9p

6s

10s

¼" seam allowance

©Lesley Brankin 2009

PUFFINS OR PUFFIN BLOCK

Foundation Papers
(reversed ready for piecing)

Fabric Key

- r: rock
- h: chest, head
- b: back, tail
- f: foot, beak
- c: contrast beak

Kindly respect my copyright and only make copies for your personal use

Piecing order for head (enlarged)

Puffins - Unit A

Puffins - Unit B*

Puffins - Unit C* 2hs*

Puffins - Unit D

Puffins - Unit E*

Puffins - Unit F* 2hs*

©Lesley Brankin 2009

* match when joining units
¼" seam allowance

Finished Block Size: 4" wide x 3" high

Finished Block
(right side facing)

48

SEAGULL BLOCK

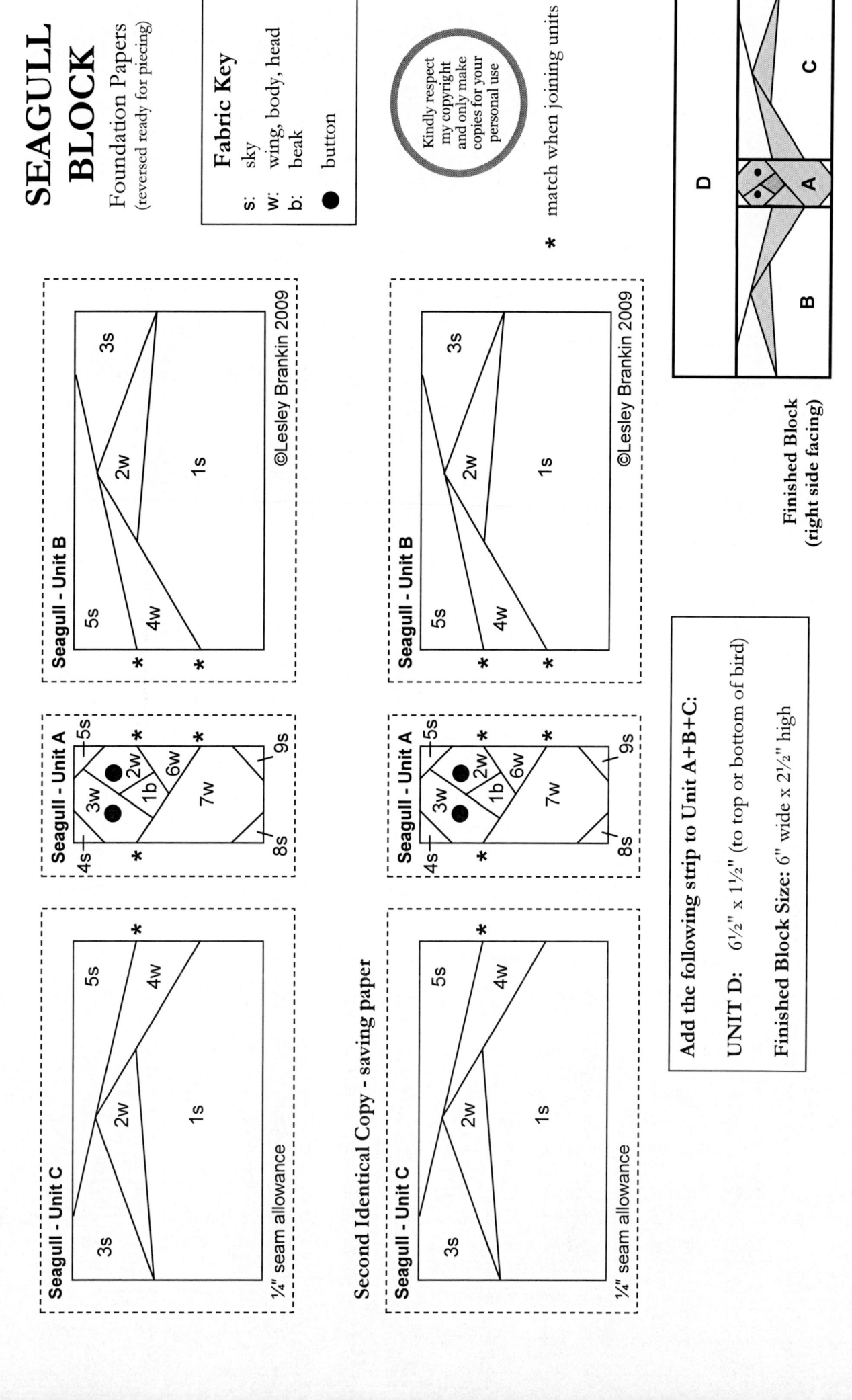

Foundation Papers (reversed ready for piecing)

Fabric Key
- s: sky
- w: wing, body, head
- b: beak
- ● button

Kindly respect my copyright and only make copies for your personal use

* match when joining units

Finished Block (right side facing)

Seagull - Unit B
- 3s
- 2w
- 1s
- 5s
- 4w

©Lesley Brankin 2009

Seagull - Unit A
- 4s, 5s
- 3w, 2w, 6w
- 1b
- 7w
- 8s, 9s

Seagull - Unit C
- 3s
- 2w
- 1s
- 5s
- 4w

¼" seam allowance

Second Identical Copy - saving paper

Seagull - Unit B
- 3s
- 2w
- 1s
- 5s
- 4w

©Lesley Brankin 2009

Seagull - Unit A
- 4s, 5s
- 3w, 2w, 6w
- 1b
- 7w
- 8s, 9s

Seagull - Unit C
- 3s
- 2w
- 1s
- 5s
- 4w

¼" seam allowance

Add the following strip to Unit A+B+C:

UNIT D: 6½" x 1½" (to top or bottom of bird)

Finished Block Size: 6" wide x 2½" high

SEAHORSES BLOCK

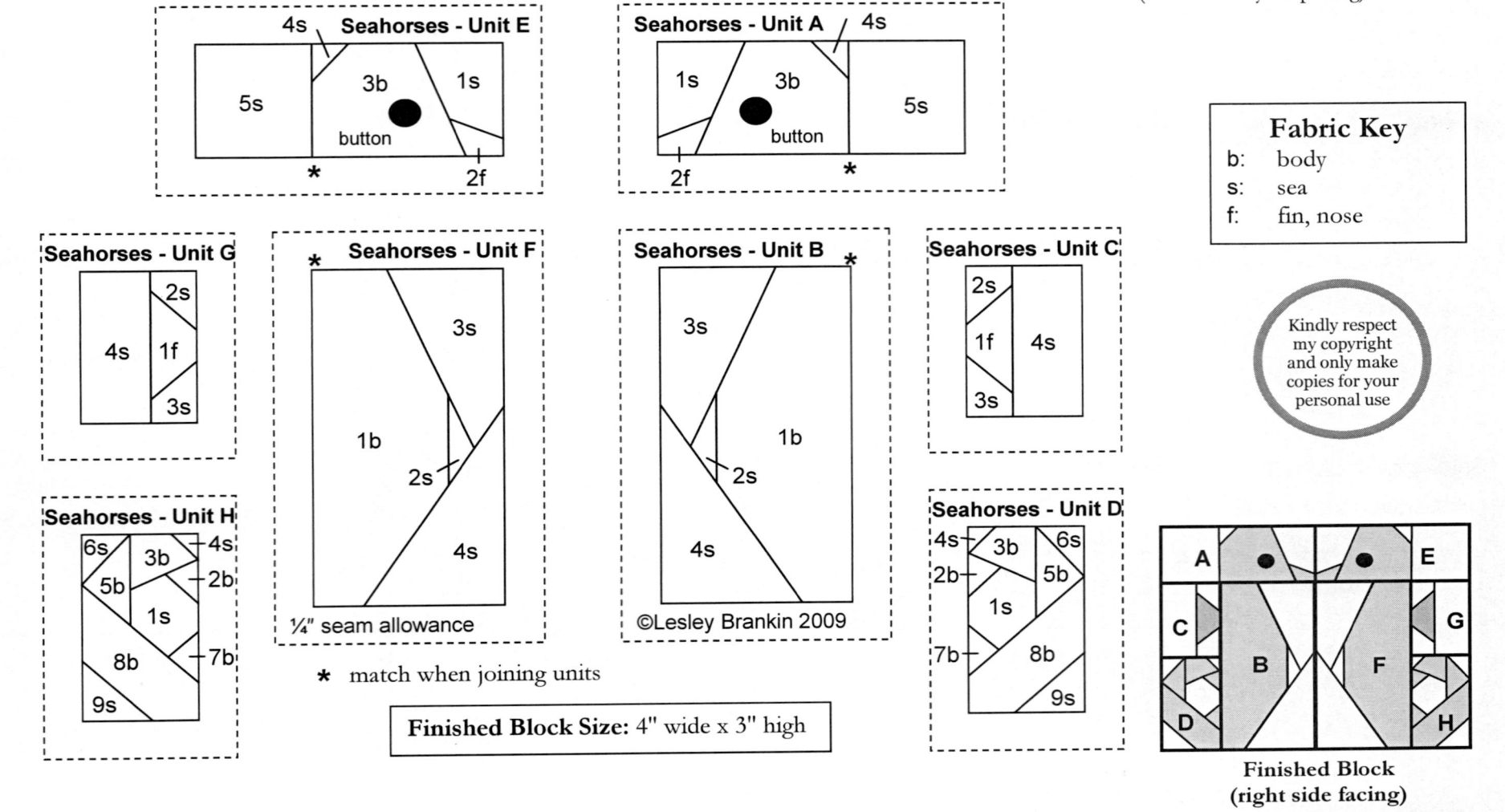

Foundation Papers
(reversed ready for piecing)

Fabric Key

- b: body
- s: sea
- f: fin, nose

Kindly respect my copyright and only make copies for your personal use

Seahorses - Unit A
Seahorses - Unit B
©Lesley Brankin 2009
Seahorses - Unit C
Seahorses - Unit D
Seahorses - Unit E
Seahorses - Unit F
¼" seam allowance
* match when joining units
Finished Block Size: 4" wide x 3" high
Seahorses - Unit G
Seahorses - Unit H

Finished Block (right side facing)

50

SEAL - BABY BLOCK

Foundation Papers
(reversed ready for piecing)

Fabric Key
r: rock
b: body

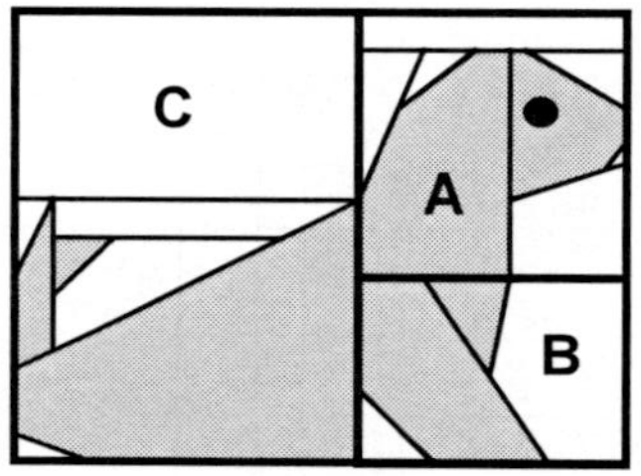

Finished Block (right side facing)

Finished Block Size: 4" wide x 3" high

Kindly respect my copyright and only make copies for your personal use

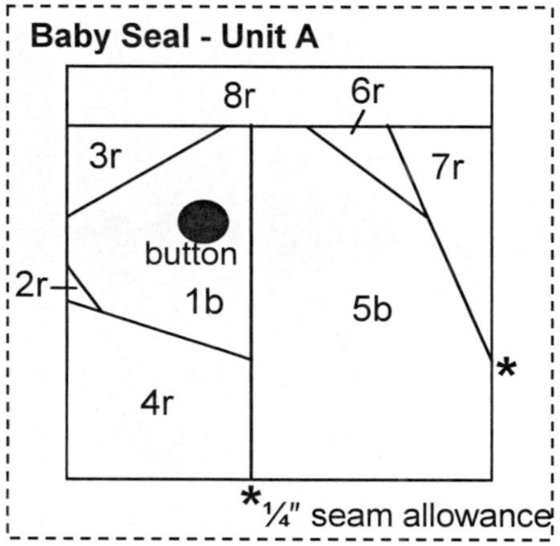

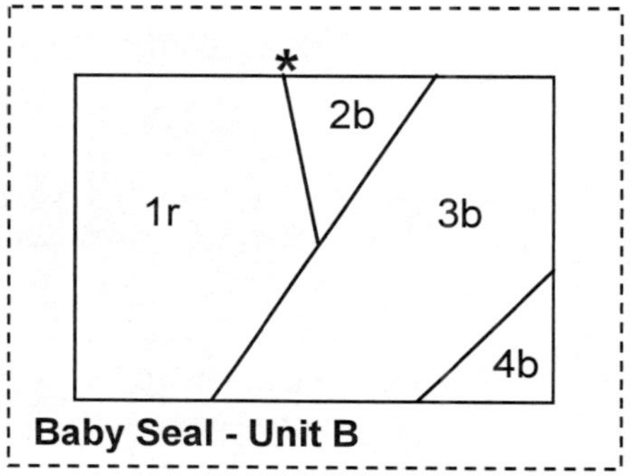

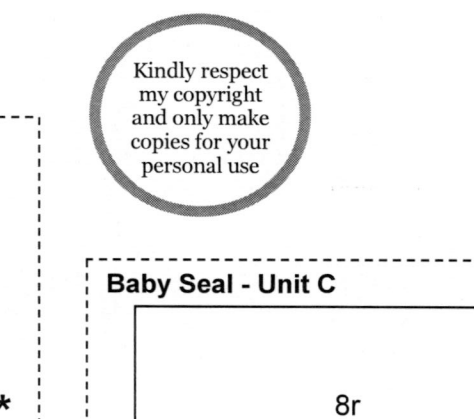

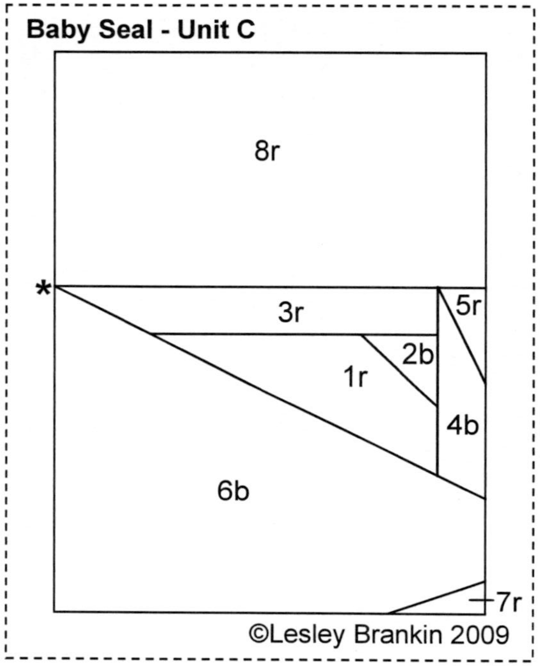

Baby Seal - Unit C

©Lesley Brankin 2009

Baby Seal - Unit A

* ¼" seam allowance

Baby Seal - Unit B

* match when joining units

SEAL - MOTHER BLOCK

Foundation Papers
(reversed ready for piecing)

Mother Seal - Unit A

¼" seam allowance

* match when joining units

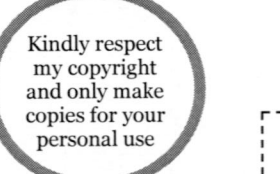

Kindly respect my copyright and only make copies for your personal use

Mother Seal - Unit B

Mother Seal - Unit C

©Lesley Brankin 2009

Fabric Key
r: rock
b: body

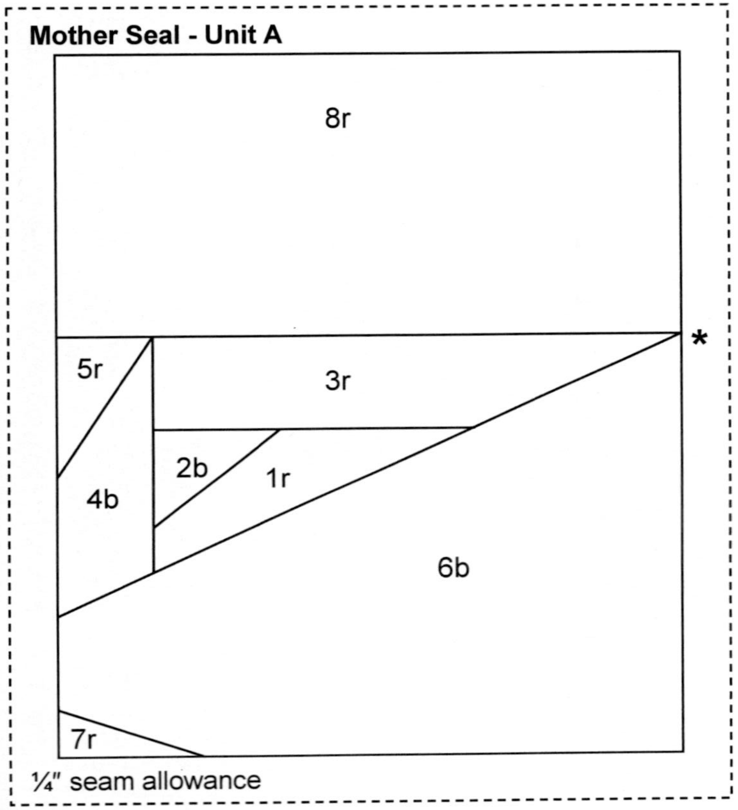

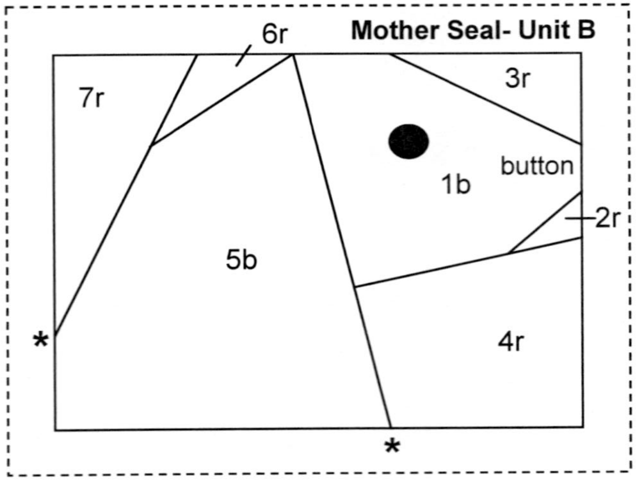

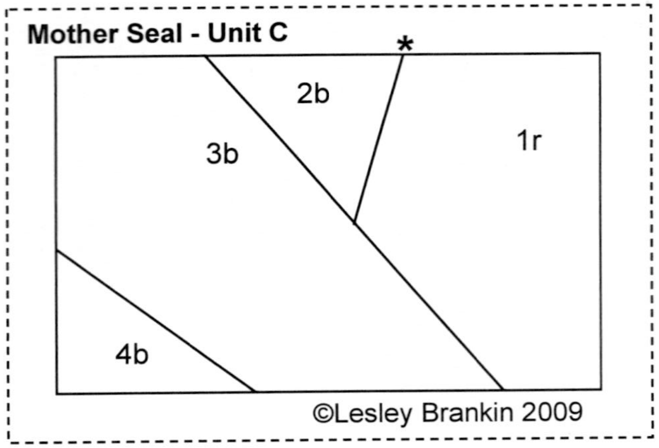

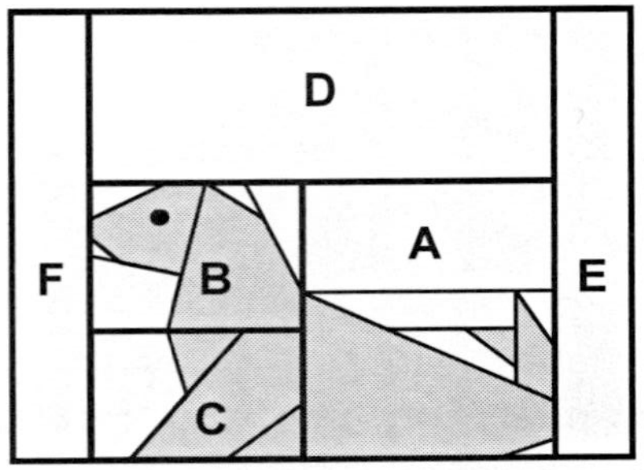

Finished Block
(right side facing)

Add the following strips to Unit A+B+C:

UNIT D: 6½" x 2¾" (to top of seal)
UNIT E: 1½" x 6½" (to right of seal)
UNIT F: 1½" x 6½" (to left of seal)

Finished Block Size: 8" wide x 6" high

52

STARFISH BLOCK

Foundation Papers
(reversed ready for piecing)

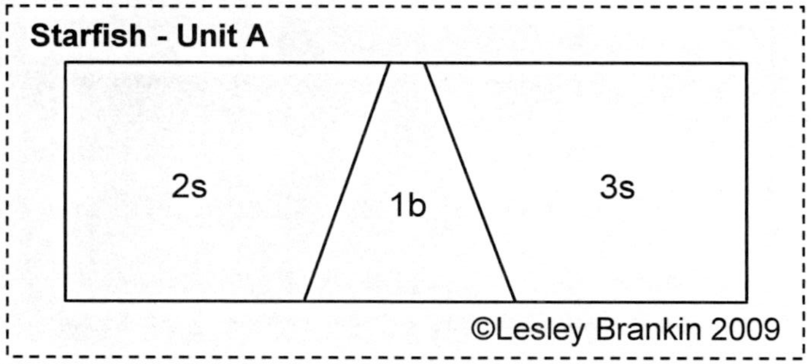

Starfish - Unit A

2s

1b

3s

©Lesley Brankin 2009

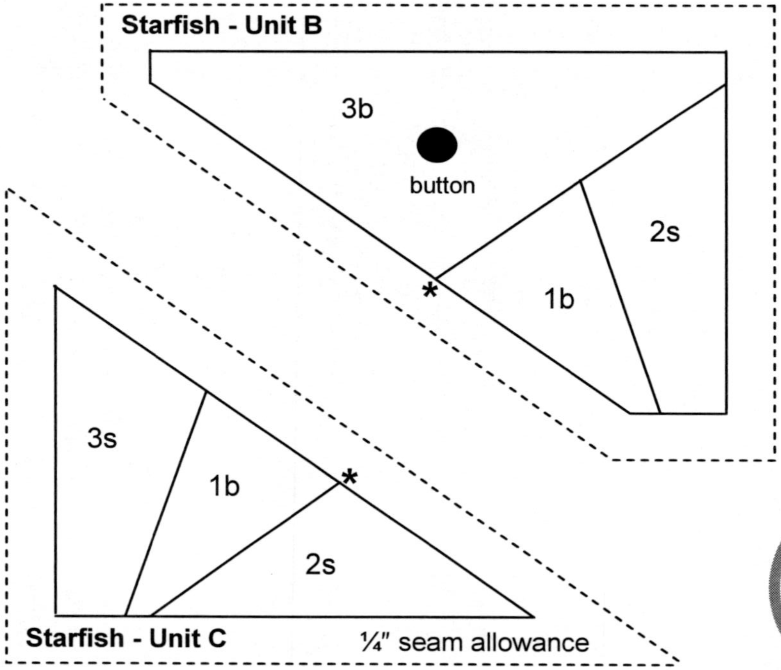

Starfish - Unit B

3b

button

1b

2s

Starfish - Unit C

3s

1b

2s

¼" seam allowance

✱ match when joining units

Kindly respect my copyright and only make copies for your personal use

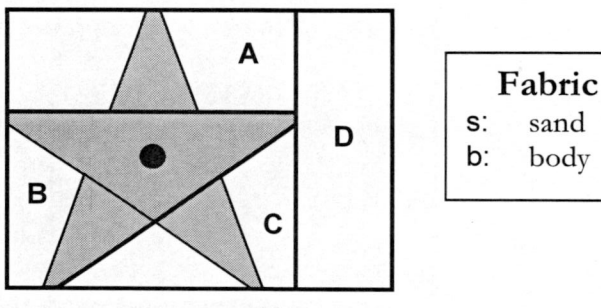

Add the following strip to Unit A+B+C:

UNIT D: 1½" x 3½" (to either side of shell)

Finished Block Size: 4" wide x 3" high

Fabric Key
s: sand
b: body

Finished Block
(right side facing)

A   D
B   C

53

SUN BLOCK

Foundation Papers
(reversed ready for piecing)

Fabric Key

- s: sky
- a: outer sun
- b: inner sun 1
- c: inner sun 2

Kindly respect my copyright and only make copies for your personal use

Make 4 sets of A and B Units

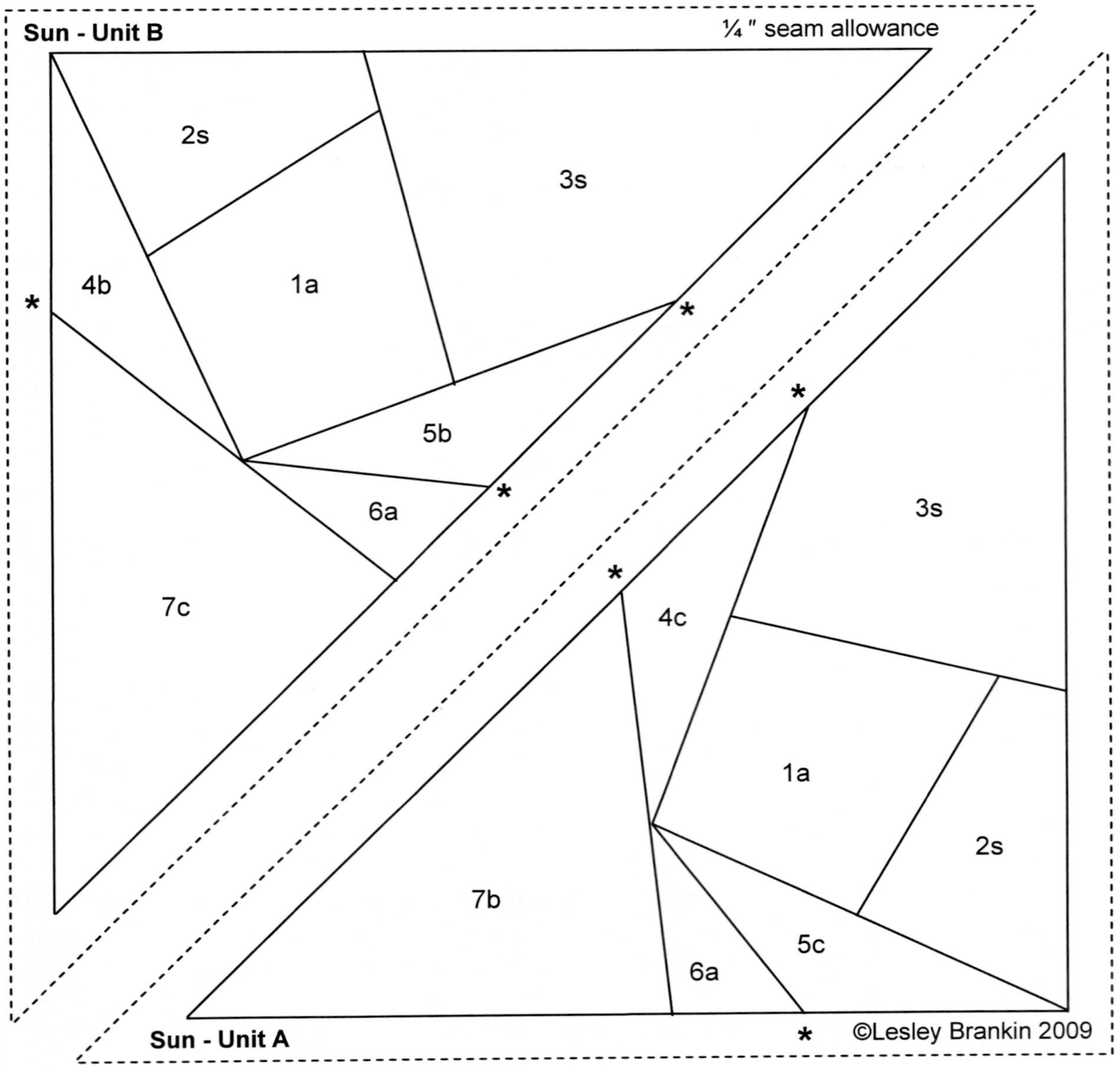

Sun - Unit B

¼" seam allowance

2s, 4b, 7c, 1a, 6a, 5b, 3s

Sun - Unit A

7b, 6a, 4c, 5c, 1a, 2s, 3s

©Lesley Brankin 2009

Finished Block Size: 10" wide x 10" high

* match when joining units

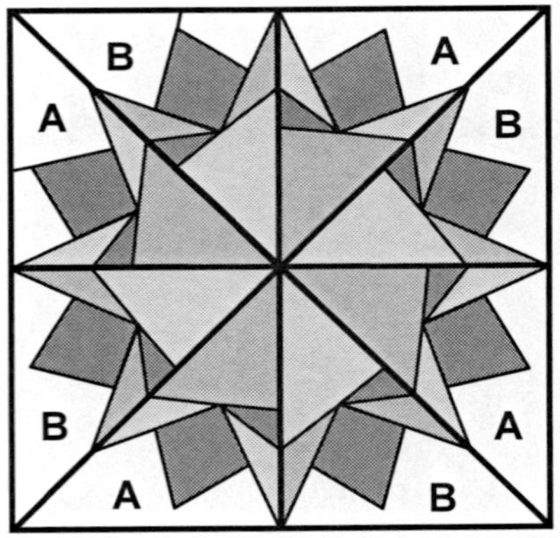

Finished Block
(right side facing)

54

TRAWLER BLOCK
Foundation Papers (reversed ready for piecing)

Trawler - Unit A

3s, 1p, 2s, 4t

Trawler - Unit B

11s, 7c, 12s, 5c, 3p, 1c, 2p, 6c, 4c, 10h, 9c, 8t

©Lesley Brankin 2009

Trawler - Unit C

2s, 1t, 4s, 3s

Trawler - Unit D

3h, 1h, 6s, 5p, 2t, 4s

¼" seam allowance

Fabric Key

- s: sky
- h: hull, roof
- c: cabin
- p: prow, windows
- t: trim, masts

Kindly respect my copyright and only make copies for your personal use

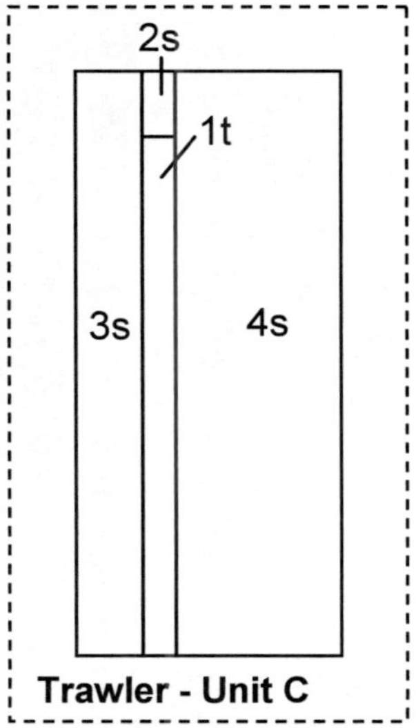

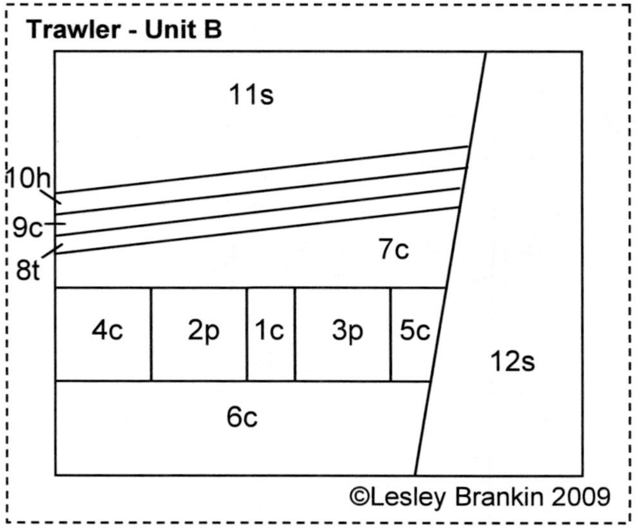

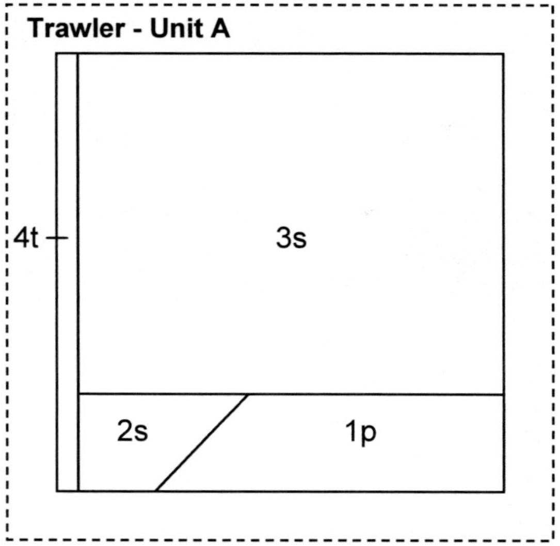

Finished Block (right side facing)

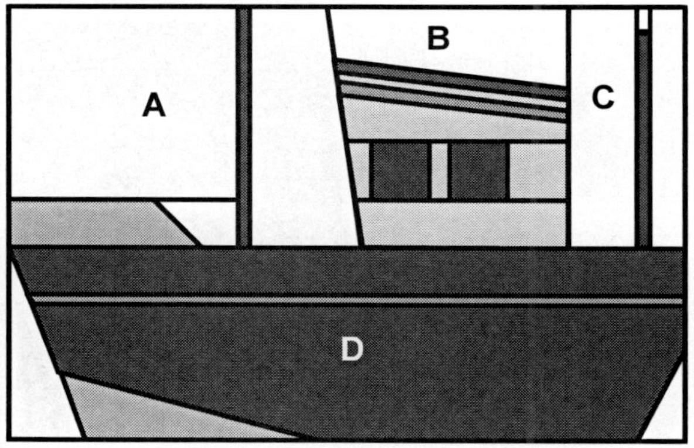

A, B, C, D

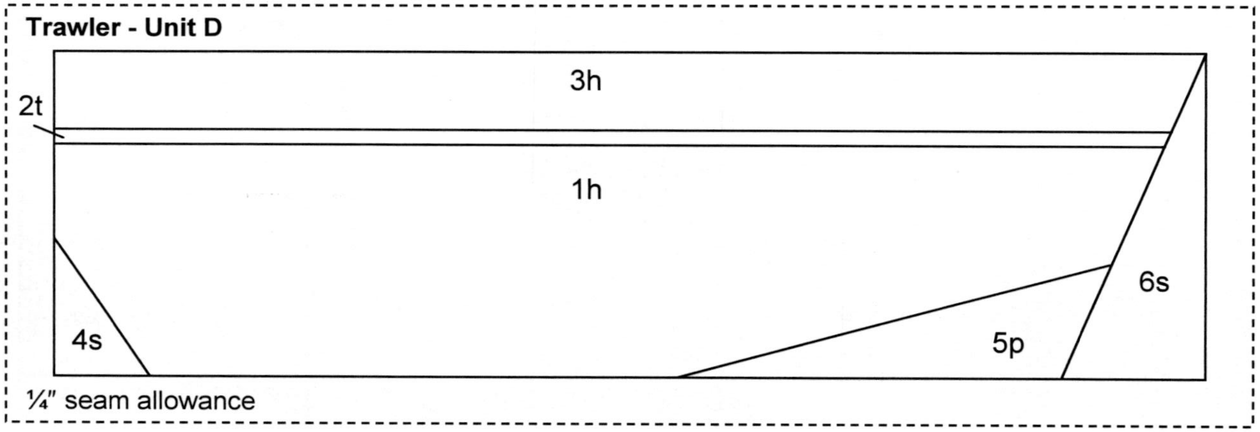

Finished Block Size: 6" wide x 4" high

TURTLE BLOCK
Foundation Papers
(reversed ready for piecing)

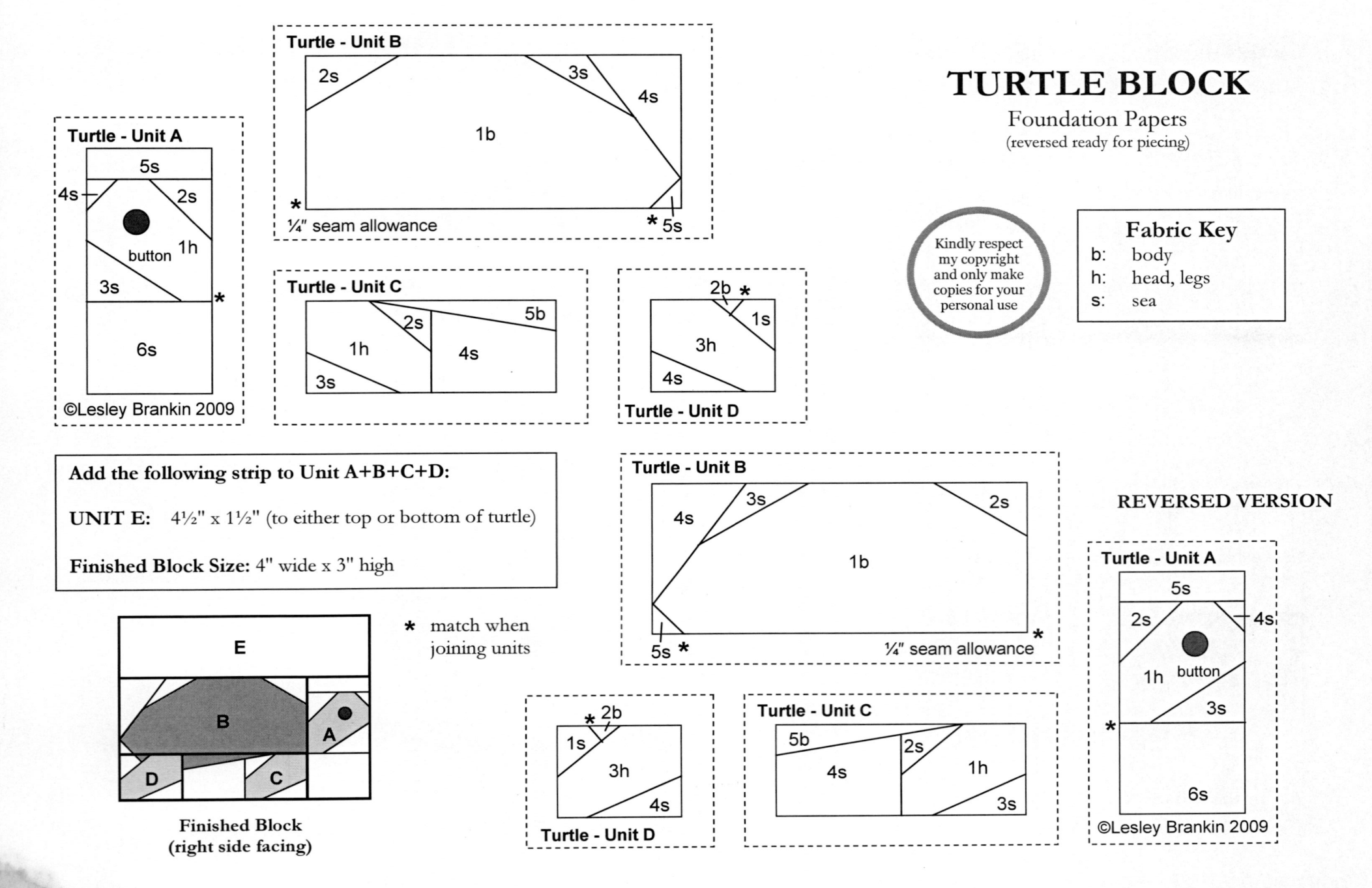

Fabric Key
b: body
h: head, legs
s: sea

Kindly respect my copyright and only make copies for your personal use

©Lesley Brankin 2009

Turtle - Unit A
4s, 5s, 3s, button 1h, 2s, 6s
*

Turtle - Unit B
2s, 1b, 3s, 4s, 5s
¼" seam allowance
*

Turtle - Unit C
3s, 1h, 2s, 4s, 5b

Turtle - Unit D
4s, 3h, 2b, 1s
*

Add the following strip to Unit A+B+C+D:
UNIT E: 4½" x 1½" (to either top or bottom of turtle)
Finished Block Size: 4" wide x 3" high

* match when joining units

Finished Block
(right side facing)

D, C, B, A, E

Turtle - Unit D
1s, 2b, 3h, 4s
*

Turtle - Unit B
5s, 4s, 3s, 1b, 2s
¼" seam allowance
*

Turtle - Unit C
5b, 4s, 2s, 1h, 3s

REVERSED VERSION

Turtle - Unit A
5s, 2s, 1h button, 3s, 4s, 6s
*
©Lesley Brankin 2009

56

WHALE BLOCK
Page 1 of 2
Foundation Papers
(reversed ready for piecing)

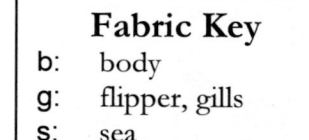

Fabric Key
- b: body
- g: flipper, gills
- s: sea

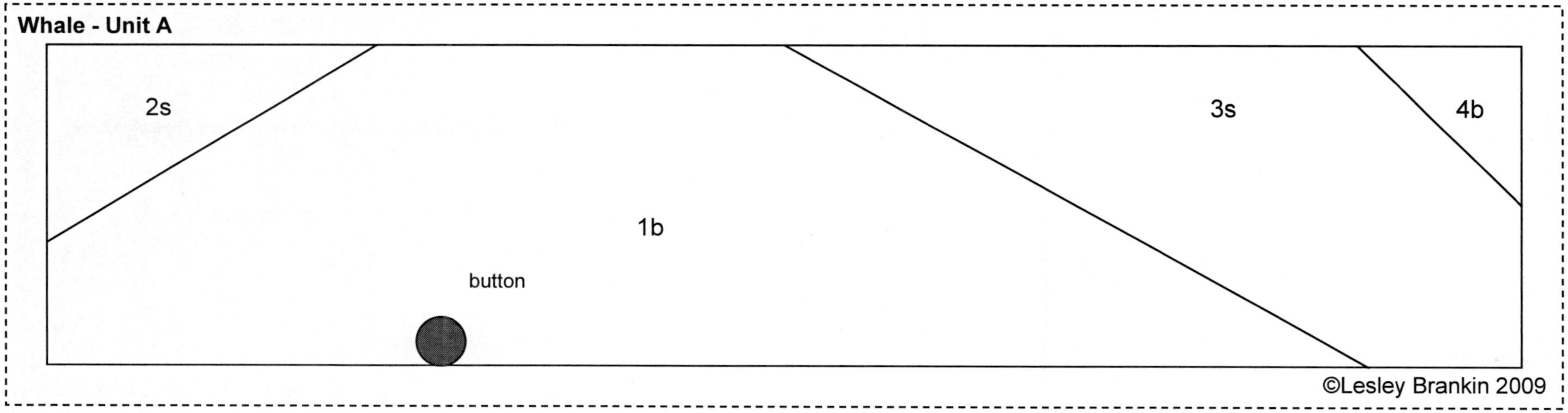

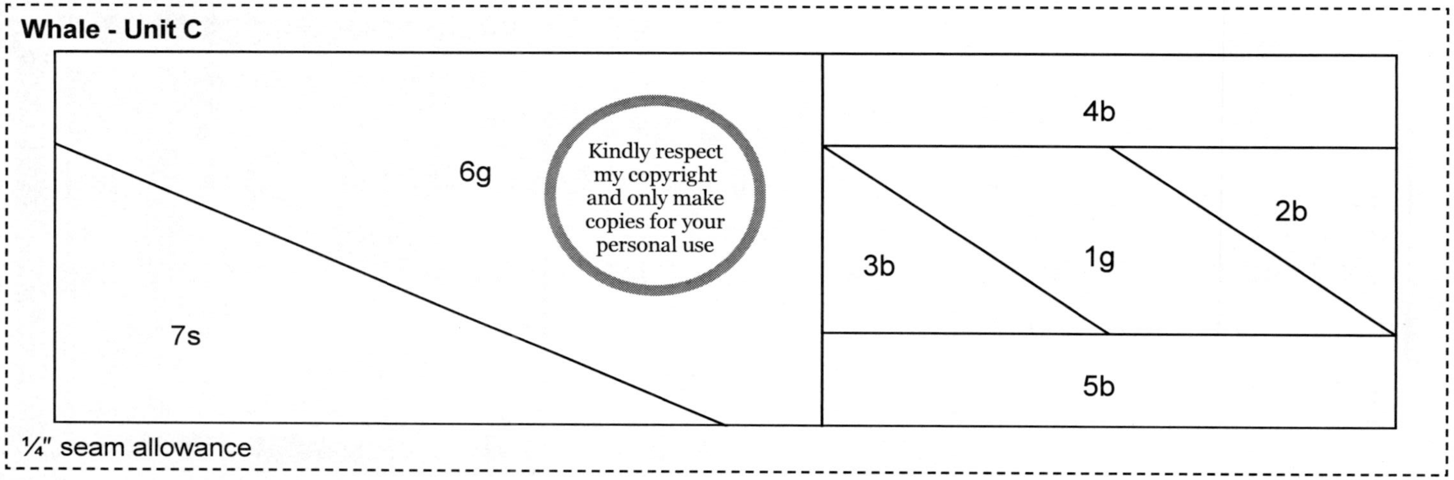

Whale - Unit A

4b
3s
1b
2s
button

©Lesley Brankin 2009

Whale - Unit C

4b
2b
1g
3b
5b
6g
7s

Kindly respect my copyright and only make copies for your personal use

¼" seam allowance

WHALE BLOCK
Page 2 of 2

Foundation Papers
(reversed ready for piecing)

* match when joining units

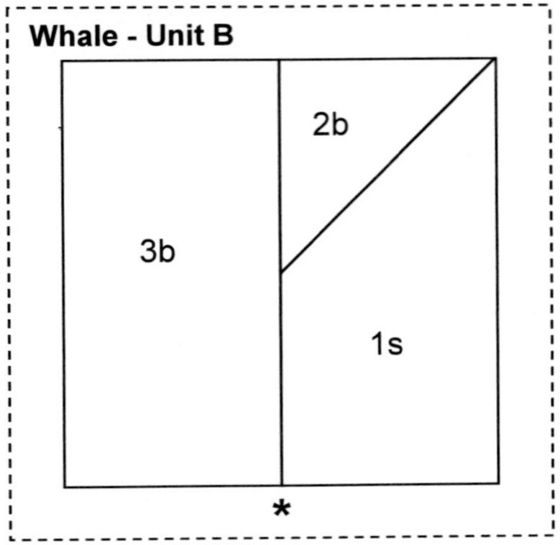

Fabric Key
- b: body
- g: flipper, gills
- s: sea

Whale - Unit B

- 3b
- 2b
- 1s

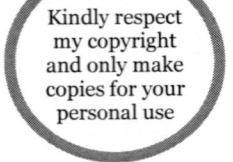

Whale - Unit D

- 1b
- 2s
- 3s

¼" seam allowance

©Lesley Brankin 2009

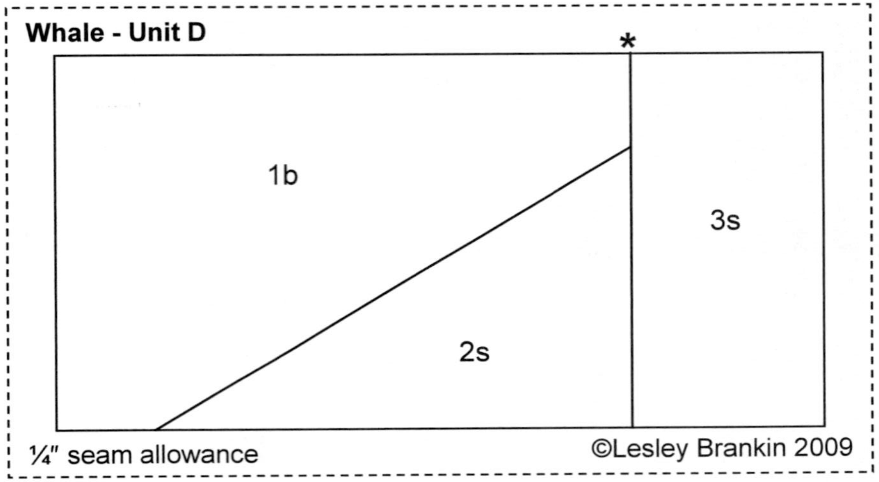

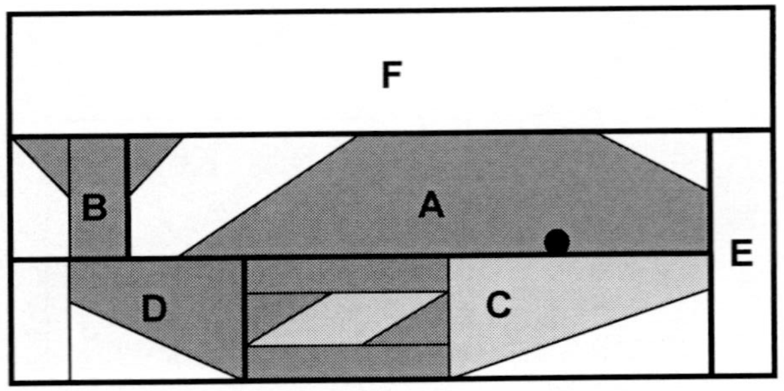

Finished Block
(right side facing)

Units: F, B, D, A, C, E

Add the following strips to Unit A+B+C+D:

UNIT E: 1½" x 4½" (to right of whale)
UNIT F: 12½" x 2½" (to top of whale)

Finished Block Size: 12" wide x 6" high

Kindly respect my copyright and only make copies for your personal use

YACHT BLOCK

Foundation Papers
(reversed ready for piecing)

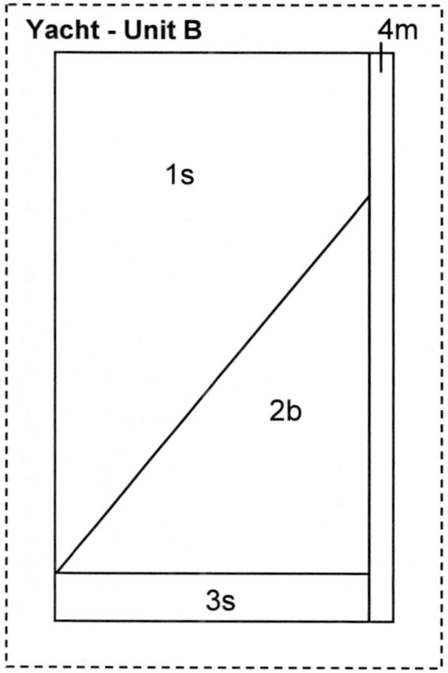

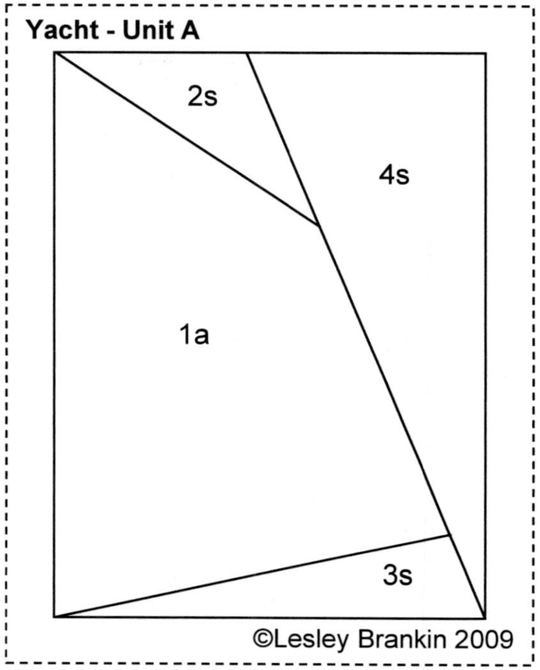

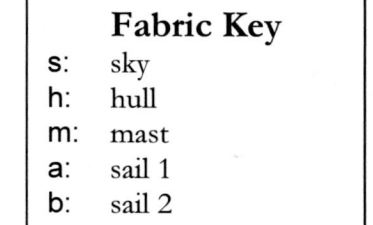

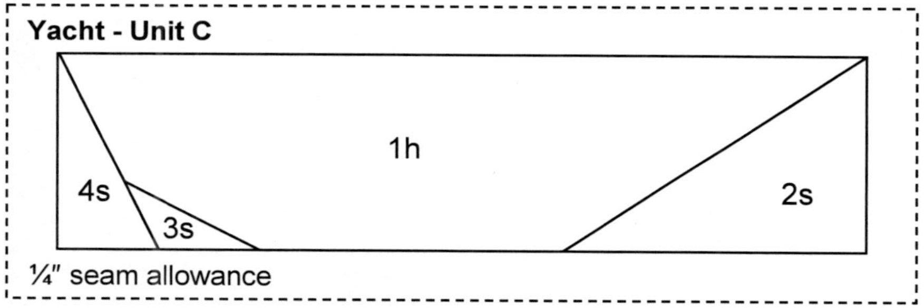

Fabric Key
- s: sky
- h: hull
- m: mast
- a: sail 1
- b: sail 2

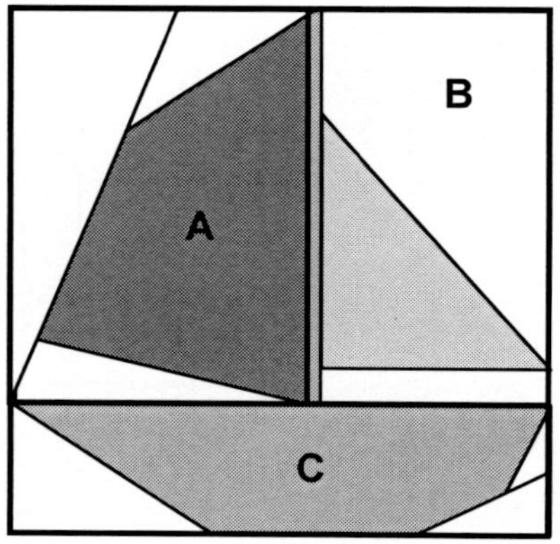

Finished Block
(right side facing)

Finished Block Size: 4" wide x 4" high

Yacht - Unit A

2s, 4s, 3s, 1a

©Lesley Brankin 2009

Yacht - Unit B

1s, 2b, 3s, 4m

Yacht - Unit C

2s, 1h, 3s, 4s

¼" seam allowance

Kindly respect my copyright and only make copies for your personal use

59

ALPHABET BLOCKS
Page 1 of 5
Foundation papers
(reversed ready for piecing)

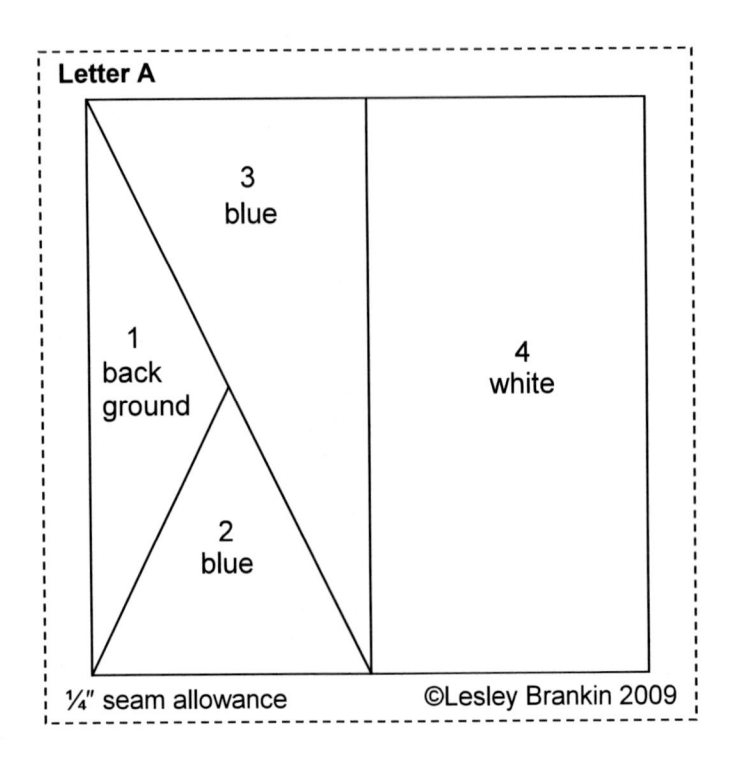

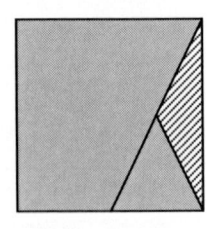

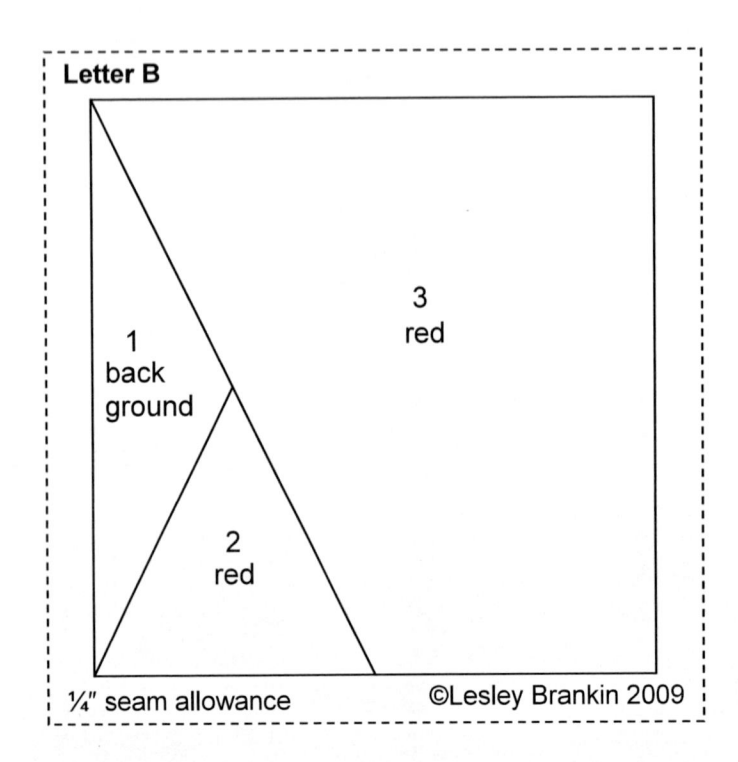

Letter A

1 background
2 blue
3 blue
4 white

¼" seam allowance ©Lesley Brankin 2009

Letter A

Kindly respect my copyright and only make copies for your personal use

Letter B

Letter B

1 background
2 red
3 red

¼" seam allowance ©Lesley Brankin 2009

ALPHABET BLOCKS
Page 2 of 5
Foundation papers
(reversed ready for piecing)

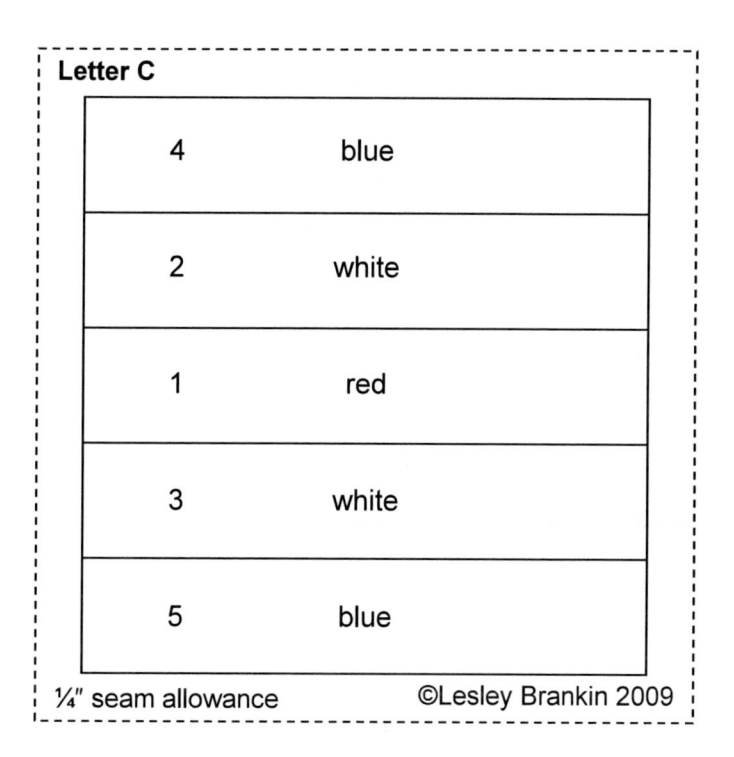

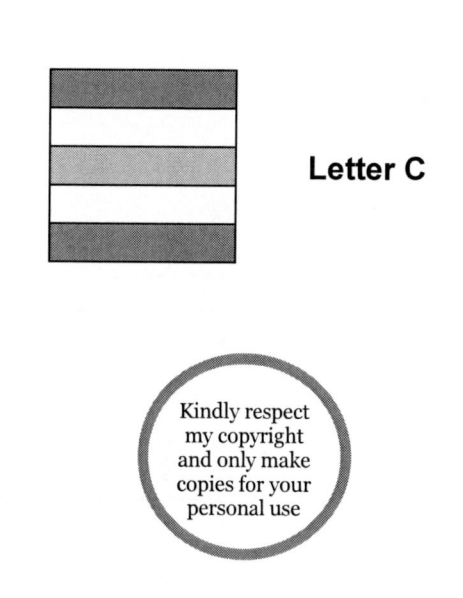

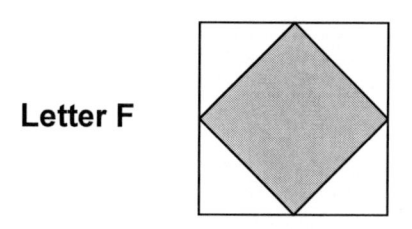

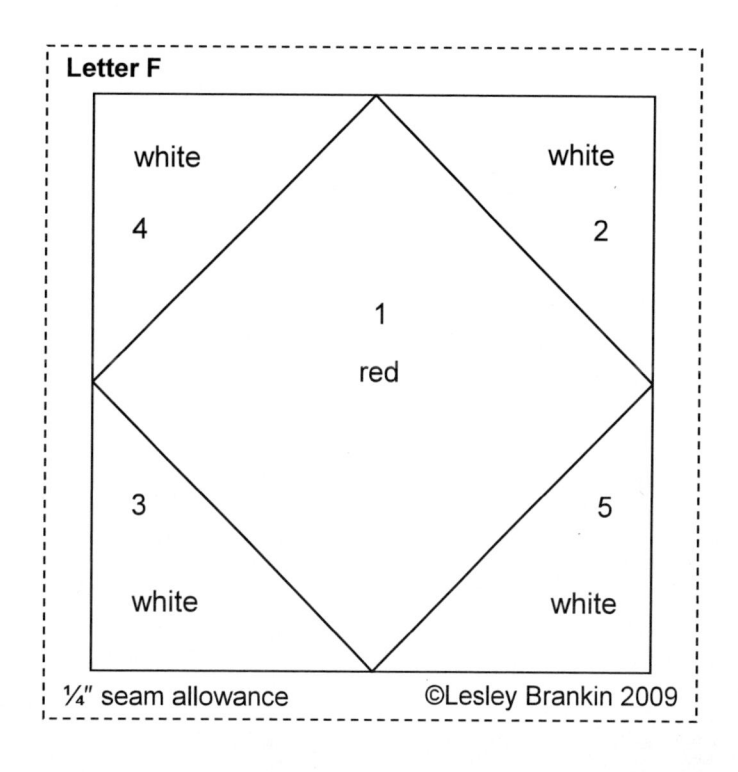

Letter C

4	blue
2	white
1	red
3	white
5	blue

¼" seam allowance ©Lesley Brankin 2009

Letter C

Kindly respect my copyright and only make copies for your personal use

Letter F

Letter F

- white 4
- white 2
- 1 red
- 3 white
- 5 white

¼" seam allowance ©Lesley Brankin 2009

61

ALPHABET BLOCKS
Page 3 of 5
Foundation papers
(reversed ready for piecing)

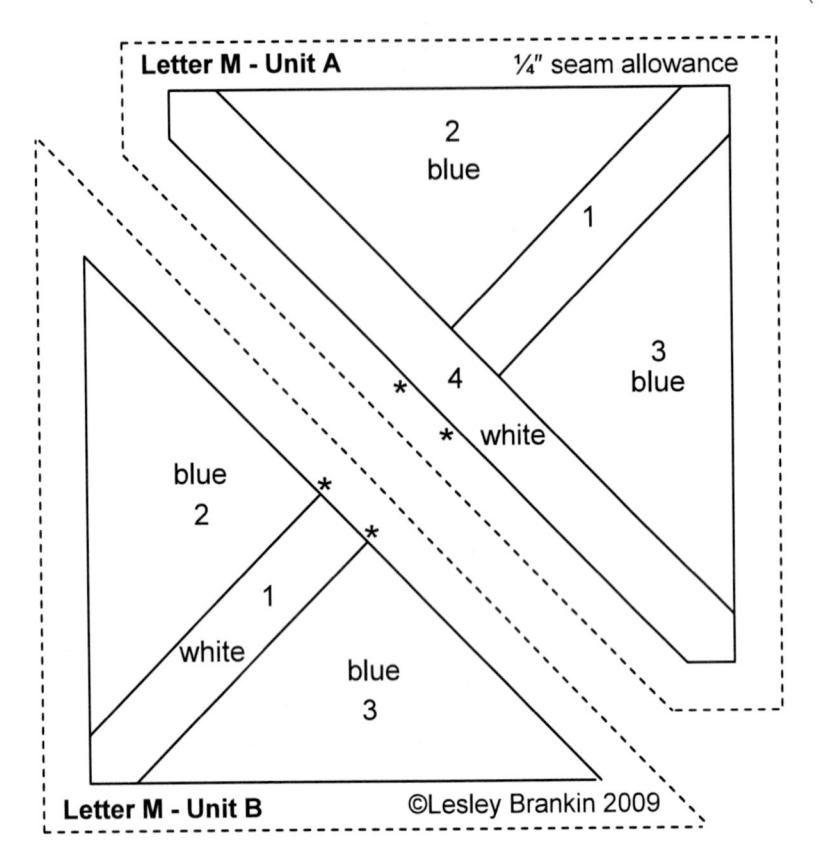

Letter M - Unit A — ¼" seam allowance
- 2 blue
- 1
- 3 blue
- 4
- white

Letter M - Unit B
- blue 2
- 1 white
- blue 3

©Lesley Brankin 2009

Letter M

Kindly respect my copyright and only make copies for your personal use

Letter V

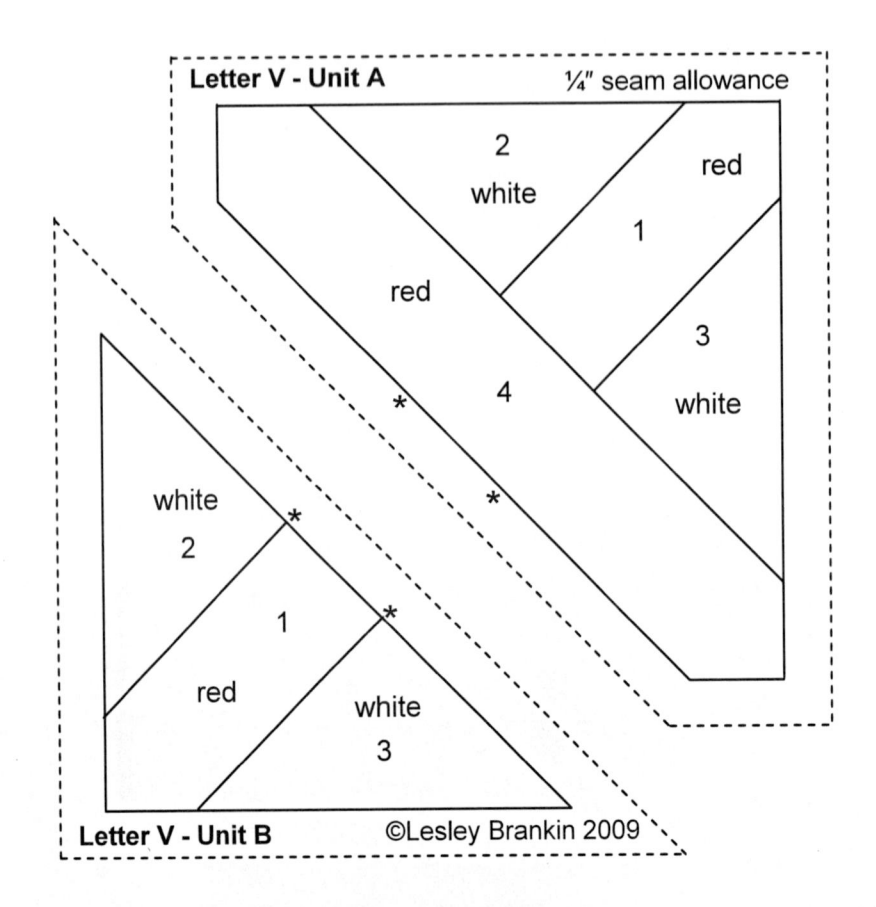

Letter V - Unit A — ¼" seam allowance
- 2 white
- red
- 1
- red
- 3 white
- 4

Letter V - Unit B
- white 2
- 1
- red
- white 3

©Lesley Brankin 2009

ALPHABET BLOCKS
Page 4 of 5
Foundation papers
(reversed ready for piecing)

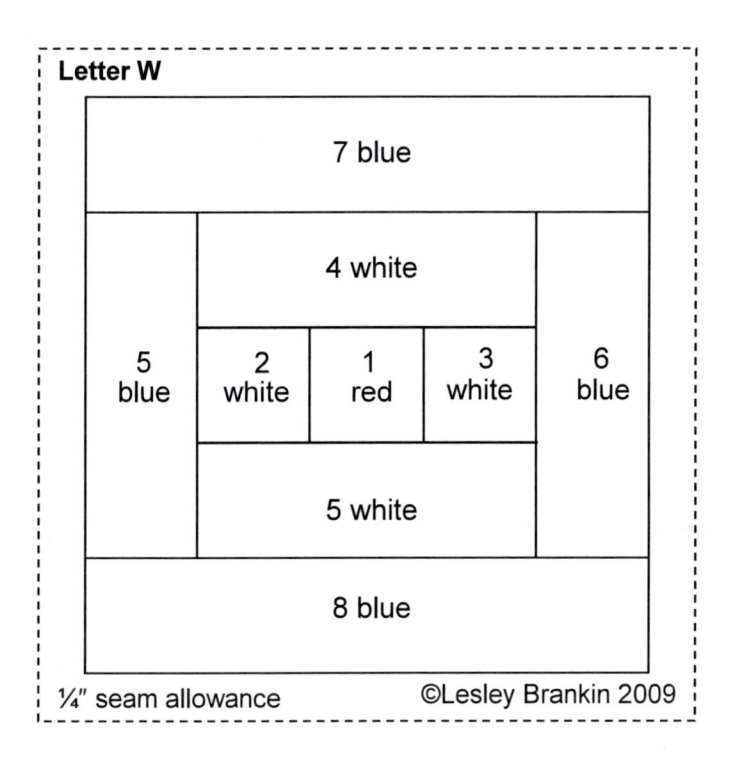

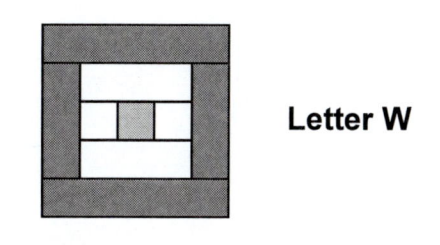

Letter W

	7 blue			
	4 white			
5 blue	2 white	1 red	3 white	6 blue
	5 white			
	8 blue			

¼" seam allowance ©Lesley Brankin 2009

Letter W

Kindly respect my copyright and only make copies for your personal use

Letter Y

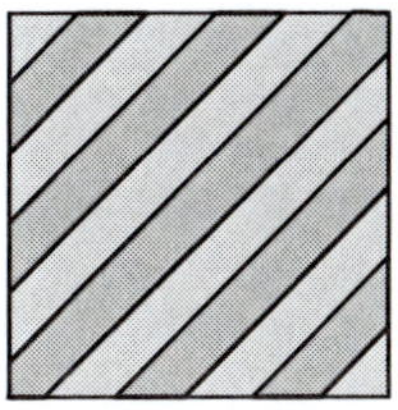

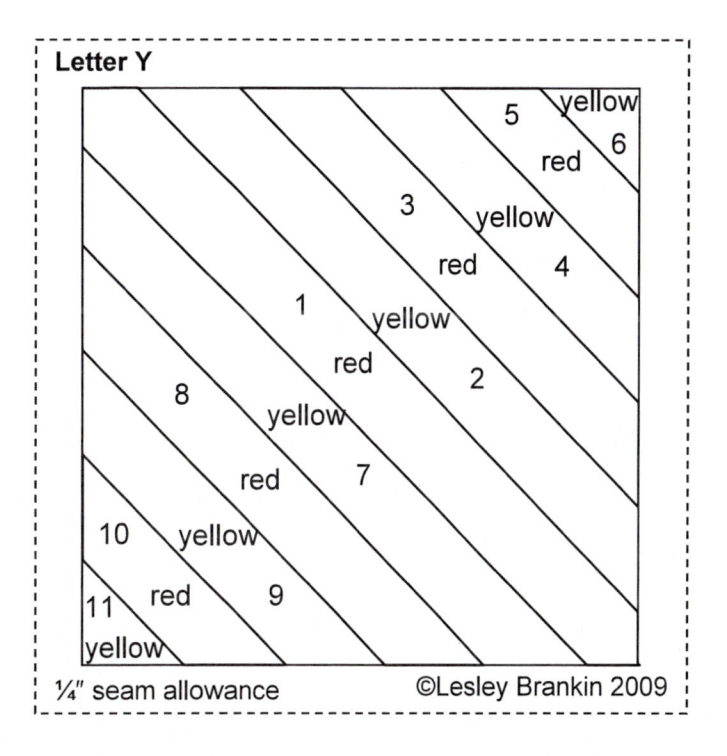

Letter Y

5 yellow
6 red
3 yellow
red 4
1 yellow
red 2
8 yellow
red 7
10 yellow
11 red 9
yellow

¼" seam allowance ©Lesley Brankin 2009

63

ALPHABET BLOCKS
Page 5 of 5
Foundation papers
(reversed ready for piecing)

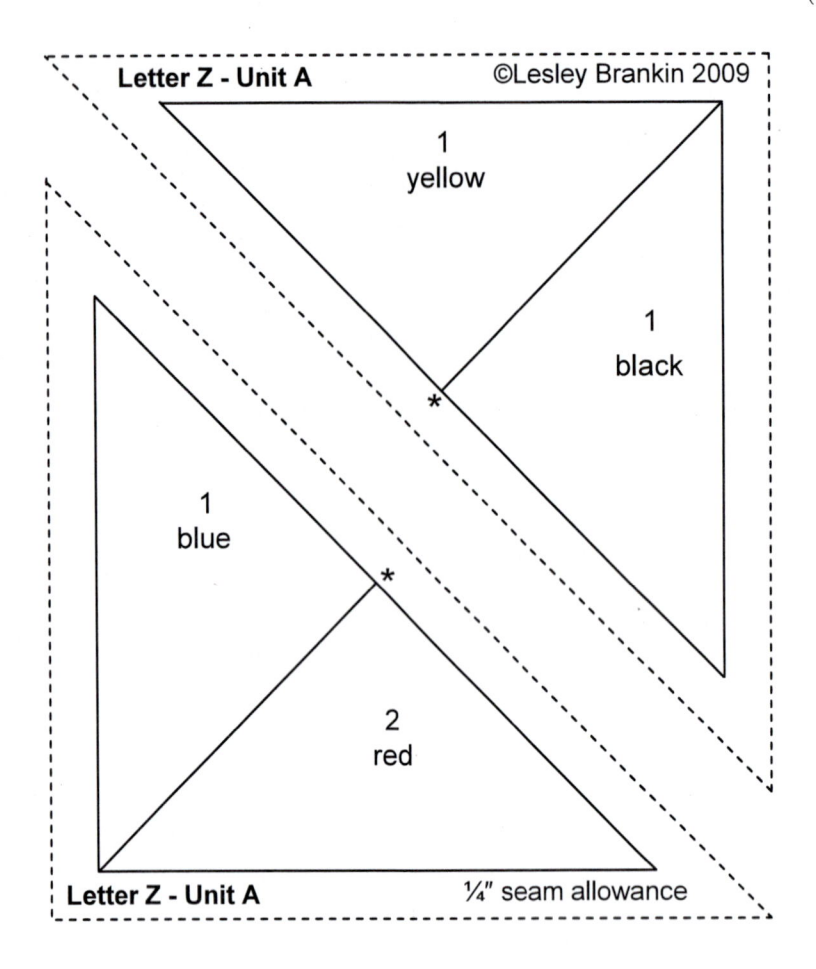

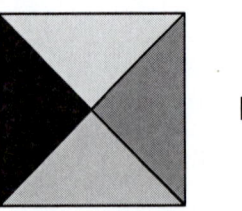

Letter Z - Unit A
©Lesley Brankin 2009

1 yellow

1 black

1 blue

2 red

Letter Z - Unit A   ¼" seam allowance

Letter Z

Kindly respect my copyright and only make copies for your personal use